The Deadly Dozen
Volume Two
12 More of America's
Worst Serial Killers

Robert Keller

Please Leave Your Review of This Book At http://bit.ly/kellerbooks

ISBN-13: 978-1534800847

ISBN-10: 1534800840

© 2016 by Robert Keller

robertkellerauthor.com

All rights reserved.

No part of this publication may be copied or reproduced in any format, electronic or otherwise, without the prior, written consent of the copyright holder and publisher. This book is for informational and entertainment purposes only and the author and publisher will not be held responsible for the misuse of information contain herein, whether deliberate or incidental.

Much research, from a variety of sources, has gone into the compilation of this material. To the best knowledge of the author and publisher, the material contained herein is factually correct. Neither the publisher, nor author will be held responsible for any inaccuracies.

Table of Contents

Who makes the list? 5

Rodney Alcala 7

Kenneth Bianchi & Angelo Buono 17

Larry Eyler 29

Donald 'Pee Wee' Gaskins 39

H.H. Holmes 51

Patrick Kearney 63

Edmund Kemper 73

Bobby Joe Long 83

Earle Nelson 95

Joel Rifkin 105

Arthur Shawcross 115

Coral Eugene Watts 125

What Makes A Serial Killer? 135

12 More of America's Worst Serial Killers

Who makes the list?

When I originally sat down to write *The Deadly Dozen: America's 12 Worst Serial Killers*, I was faced with a quandary. Which cases to include and which to leave out? Compiling any such "Best of" or "Worst of" list is, of course, highly subjective, but I was determined to put together a collective that had some firm criteria behind it.

But what criteria?

The most obvious one would be number of victims. Surely the worst serial killers had to be those who had claimed the most victims? But as I soon found out, this idea was problematic. Which number do you use? The number of murders a killer has been convicted of? The number he has confessed to? The number that he is suspected of? For one reason or another, none of these is an accurate depiction.

And are victim numbers the best criteria for ranking such a list anyway? What about level of depravity? What about degree of infamy? Slightly nebulous, I know, but should they not play a part?

In the end, I was forced to concede that any list that I put together would be based, to some degree at least, on my particular biases. Inevitably, the cases would be the one's that fascinated or frightened me.

And so, *The Deadly Dozen* went to market and inevitably attracted it comments about the cases I'd chosen to cover. There were also plenty of ideas about cases that might have been included, as well as suggestions that those might form the basis for a second book. This then, is that book.

Once again, I've been somewhat subjective in my choices, selecting those that   strike a chord with me. Generally, these qualify under the same criteria as used in the first book; victim count, level of depravity, level of infamy, and "degree of creepiness," the ability of a case to get under one's skin.

But even as I write this, I realize that I've had to omit a number of notorious cases that might have made the cut. Cases like those of Robert Hansen, the Alaskan sicko who hunted his victims like animals; or David Carpenter, San Francisco's scary Trailside Killer, or Bittaker and Norris, surely one of the most depraved "killer teams" in history. Then there's Lake and Ing, Sunset Strip Slayer Douglas Clark, and disgusting child murderer Westley Allan Dodd, to name but a few.

All of these cases feature in my *American Monsters* series of books but for one reason or another, they are not included here. These are the ones that are.

Rodney Alcala

The Dating Game Killer

In September 1978, a handsome young man by the name of Rodney Alcala appeared as a contestant on a popular TV game show. He was articulate and witty, his somewhat crude brand of humor perfectly suited to the new, racy format of The Dating Game. The smooth-talking Alcala won that episode and earned a dinner with pretty bachelorette Cheryl Bradshaw, although she later declined to go on the date. It was a wise move on her part. Although Bradshaw couldn't have known it at the time, Rodney Alcala was a serial killer. By the time he made that appearance on The Dating Game, he had already raped and murdered at least five women.

Rodney James Alcala was born in San Antonio, Texas, in 1943. His father abandoned the family while Rodney was still a boy and he and his two sisters were raised by their mother who later moved them to Los Angeles. There, Alcala attended high school, graduating in 1960 at age 17.

After leaving school, the young Alcala opted for a career in the military and joined the Army, where he served as a clerk. Four years later, he suffered a nervous breakdown resulting in his eventual discharge on medical grounds. That was in 1964 and already the first warning signs had appeared. An army psychiatrist described Alcala as an anti-social personality type.

Alcala returned to L.A. At a loose end, he decided to go back to school and enrolled in a Fine Arts course at UCLA. Four years later, in 1968, he emerged with a Bachelor's degree and a near obsessive interest in photography, something that he'd soon put to sinister use.

The year after he graduated, Alcala had his first run-in with the law. A passerby spotted him luring an 8-year-old girl into his car and followed him as he drove the child back to his apartment. After Alcala took the girl inside, the concerned citizen called the police. By the time officers arrived on the scene, Alcala had already knocked the girl unconscious with a metal pipe and was raping her. When they banged on the door, he climbed through a rear window and escaped, leaving the child lying on the bed, comatose and surrounded by photography equipment. She would almost certainly have died had the bystander not alerted the police.

With a warrant out for his arrest, Alcala fled to New York, where he adopted the name, John Berger. Not that he made any attempt to lay low. He was soon hobnobbing with Manhattan's in-crowd, attending New York University, and taking a film class taught by acclaimed director Roman Polanski. The handsome Alcala had a steady stream of lovers during this time but, of course, that was not enough for a predator like him. On June 12, 1971, he committed his first known murder.

The victim was a 23-year-old TWA flight attendant named Cornelia Crilley. Detectives would later develop the theory that Alcala had befriended Crilley by helping her move into her 83rd Street apartment. He then began pestering her for sex but she turned him down as she had a boyfriend. Alcala responded in typical fashion, raping and murdering the woman.

This theory, however, would only come later, when Alcala was in custody on other charges. For the time being, Crilley's boyfriend, Leon Borstein, was the main suspect, with Alcala not even on the radar. He, in any case, had absconded for New Hampshire, where he took a job as a counselor at a drama camp near Lake Sunapee.

The prospect of a sexual predator like Rodney Alcala overseeing a group of teenaged girls is a frightening one. Fortunately, a chance set of circumstances was about to unmask him for the miscreant he was. During a summer storm, two camp attendees took shelter from the rain inside the local post office. There they saw a poster for a man named Rodney Alcala, wanted in connection with the rape of a child in Los Angeles. It struck the girls that Alcala bore a remarkable resemblance to their camp counselor, John Berger. When the storm subsided, the girls walked directly to the local sheriff's office and reported their suspicions.

Alcala was taken into custody and held until he could be extradited to California. There, he was found guilty of kidnapping, rape, and assault, although the punishment hardly fit the crime. For the brutal rape that would no doubt scar his young victim for life, Alcala served just 34 months.

And that brief prison spell did nothing to discourage Alcala from his criminal behavior. Back on the streets in 1974, he was soon up to his old tricks again. After kidnapping a 13-year-old girl, he drove her to an isolated spot near Bolsa Chica State Beach, where he forced her to smoke marijuana and then tried to rape her. The girl escaped and called the police. Alcala, still on parole for his previous attack on a minor, got another lenient sentence - just two years.

After he got out, Alcala charmed his parole officer into allowing him to visit relatives in New York. This was in the summer of 1977, the summer of Sam, when David Berkowitz was creating havoc on the streets of New York City. Alcala soon added his own brand of mayhem to the mix.

During the summer that Alcala spent in New York, 23-year-old heiress, Ellen Hover, disappeared. Ellen, daughter of Herman Hover, the owner of legendary Hollywood nightclub, Ciro's, was last seen on July 15, 1977. Her datebook for that day showed that she had an appointment to meet with "John Berger."

The disappearance of such a prominent person was big news in New York and a massive effort was launched to find her. When the police appeared to be making little headway in the case, the Hover family hired a team of private investigators and also took out a full-page ad in the New York Times, asking for information about the mysterious John Berger. Neither of these efforts produced any results because "Berger" was back in L.A., working as a typesetter for the Los Angeles Times and using his real name, Rodney Alcala.

It wasn't until a year later that the authorities linked the "John Berger" wanted in New York, with the man who'd been arrested in New Hampshire a few years before, under the same name. It was then a simple matter for FBI agents to track Alcala to Los Angeles. But finding him and proving murder were two different things entirely. Alcala admitted that he'd known Ellen, but denied having anything to do with her disappearance. Without evidence to the contrary, investigators had no option but to let him go.

(Ellen Hover's body would eventually be found buried on the Rockefeller estate in North Tarrytown, New York, just yards from where Alcala had once held a photo shoot with an aspiring model)

Back in Los Angeles, Rodney Alcala wasn't the only predator on the streets. This was at the height of the Hillside Strangler murders, and with the strangled bodies of young woman turning up with horrific regularity, the city was living under a state of virtual siege. Alcala's next victim, in fact, was at first thought to have been killed by the elusive strangler.

Jill Barcomb was an 18-year-old runaway, originally from Brooklyn, New York. At barely five-feet tall and weighing less than 100 pounds she looked younger than her age, and perhaps that is what attracted Alcala to her. He picked her up on Sunset

Boulevard and drove her into the Hollywood Hills. There he raped her, beat her on the head with a rock, and finally strangled her to death. Then he posed her in an explicit kneeling position. Her body was discovered by a film crew in November 1977.

Just a month later, Georgia Wixted, a 27-year-old nurse, was discovered dead in her Malibu apartment. The previous evening, she'd driven a co-worker home from a bar. When she didn't show up for work the next day, the co-worker reported her missing. Police arrived at her apartment to find signs of forced entry. Georgia Wixted was found naked and posed in a kneeling position on her bedroom floor. She'd been strangled, and her skull had been caved in with a hammer. She'd also been sexually assaulted and her genitals had been mutilated.

Six months later, Alcala struck again. In June 1978, Charlotte Lamb, an attractive, 32-year-old legal secretary from Santa Monica, was found dead in the laundry room of her apartment building. There were many similarities to the Wixted homicide. Lamb had been raped, beaten and strangled, and was posed with her hands behind her back.

A short while after, Alcala was back in prison, serving a short term on a drug possession charge. He was also questioned by detectives from the Hillside Strangler Task Force (a matter of routine, since he was a known sex offender). By September, he was back on the streets and enjoying his 15 minutes of fame as a contestant on The Dating Game.

In February 1979, Rodney Alcala picked up a 15-year-old hitchhiker in Riverside County. He took her to his apartment where, according to his later confession, they had consensual sex. The next morning, he drove with the girl into the mountains where he took some nude photographs of her. But something made the girl panic and as she tried to get away from him, he beat and then raped her. Inexplicably, given Alcala's M.O., he later drove the girl back to Riverside and released her. She immediately reported the abduction and rape to the police. Alcala was arrested and then bailed by his mother.

Awaiting trial on the rape charge, Alcala committed two more murders in June 1979. The first was Jill Parenteau, last seen alive when she left work early to attend a baseball game. When she didn't show up the next day, friends reported her missing. Police checking on her apartment found the 21-year-old dead on her bathroom floor. She'd been sexually assaulted, beaten and strangled. Her assailant had posed her body suggestively, using pillows to prop her up. There were signs of forced entry to the apartment and her killer had cut himself climbing in through a window. Blood evidence matching only 3% of the population did not finger Rodney Alcala as the perpetrator, but it didn't rule him out either.

Just weeks later, on June 20, 1979, 12-year-old Robin Samsoe from Huntington Beach, disappeared on her way to a ballet class. Earlier in the day, Robin's neighbor, Jacky Young, had chased a man away who'd been pestering Robin and a friend, trying to get them to pose for him in their swimsuits. Several other teenaged girls testified that a man had approached them on the beach that day, asking if he could photograph them. They later identify that man as Rodney Alcala.

Twelve days after Robin Samsoe disappeared, William Poepke, a park ranger, found her decomposing remains in the foothills of the Sierra Madres. A kitchen knife was found nearby but the level of decomposition meant it was impossible to determine whether she'd been raped.

With positive identification from several witnesses putting Alcala at the scene of Robin Samsoe's abduction, police moved in and arrested him on July 24, 1979. They then obtained a search warrant for his mother's home where they found a receipt for a storage locker in Seattle. Inside the locker were hundreds of photographs of young girls. Detectives also found a pair of gold earrings matching those worn by Robin Samsoe on the day she went missing. A second pair of earrings would later be found to carry traces of Charlotte Lamb's DNA.

With the evidence from the storage locker and the testimony of several eyewitnesses, prosecutors brought Alcala to trial for the murder of Robin Samsoe. Alcala claimed an alibi, one that was backed up by his mother and two sisters. He claimed that he had been at Knott's Berry Farm that day, applying for a job as a photographer. Phone records were produced to prove that a call had been made from that location to his mother's house, but there was no proof that Alcala had been the one who'd actually made the call. And anyway, the jury wasn't buying it. They found Alcala guilty of first-degree murder and recommended the death penalty.

But the story doesn't end there. Alcala's conviction was overturned by the California Supreme Court in 1984. He was then retried for the same offense, again found guilty and again overturned - this time by the U.S. Supreme Court of Appeals.

Alcala must have thought he had a charmed life, must have thought (like many serial killers) that he was invincible. Unfortunately for him, his earlier crimes were about to catch up with him, courtesy of a new tool in the investigator's forensic arsenal, DNA matching.

When evidence from the Barcomb, Wixted, Lamb and Parenteau murder scenes were subjected to DNA analysis, they each provided a forensic link to Rodney Alcala. The elusive serial killer had been backed into a corner at last.

Rodney Alcala went on trial in 2010, charged with the murders of Robin Samsoe, Jill Barcomb, Georgia Wixted, Charlotte Lamb and Jill Parenteau. He conducted his own defense, producing some bizarre evidence, that included a video of his appearance on The Dating Game, and an extract from Arlo Guthrie's song, "Alice's Restaurant Massacre." He urged jurors not to seek the death penalty, warning them, "You know I'll fight it."

Fortunately, the ladies and gentlemen of the jury were not intimidated. On February 25, 2010, they found Alcala guilty on five counts of first-degree murder and recommended that he be put to death for his crimes. The judge duly complied with that recommendation.

Rodney Alcala currently resides on death row at San Quentin state prison. He has since been convicted of the New York murders of

Ellen Hover and Cornelia Crilley, drawing a sentence of 25 years to life. In addition, police in Washington and New Hampshire have linked him to unsolved homicides committed there, all of which bear his unique signature.

Kenneth Bianchi & Angelo Buono

The Hillside Stranglers

Murders happen every day in a city the size of Los Angeles. And when the victims are prostitutes, they warrant hardly a mention. The lifestyle is dangerous, those who live it, well aware of the risks. And so the murders of three hookers, strangled and dumped on a hillside in October 1977, caused no more than a ripple.

But if police and the media were blasé about those crimes, they'd soon have cause to pay attention. Close to Thanksgiving 1977, came a week of unprecedented carnage. Within just a few days, the bodies of five women and girls, the youngest just 12 years old, were found in the vicinity of Glendale-Highland Park. These were not prostitutes, but ordinary girls, abducted from their middle-class neighborhoods, raped and tortured, then strangled and dumped in the hills.

The city was stunned, the media sparked into a frenzy of graphic reportage. The term "Hillside Strangler" was coined and entered everyday conversation. A serial killer was on the loose. Or rather, a pair of serial killers, because experienced detectives believed right from the start that they were looking, not for one man, but for two, working together.

On November 20, 1977, LAPD homicide detective Bob Grogan was called to the site of a murder, on a hillside somewhere between Glendale and Eagle Rock. The victim was Kristina Weckler, a 20-year-old honors student at the Pasadena Art Center of Design. She'd been raped and sodomized and then strangled. The ligature marks on her wrists, ankles, and neck, and the bruises on her breasts bore witness to torture.

While Grogan examined the crime scene, his partner, Dudley Varney, had been called to another gruesome find, two victims this time, their bodies in the early stages of decomposition, already infested by insects. The victims would later be identified as Dolores Cepeda, 12, and Sonja Johnson, 14. They'd last been seen getting off a bus and going over to talk to a man sitting in a large sedan. Witness reports that there was a person sitting in the passenger seat of the vehicle supported the police theory that there were two killers.

Then, on November 23, another young victim was found, this time near the Los Feliz off ramp on the Golden State Freeway. The level of decomposition suggested that the woman had been there two weeks but made it impossible to determine whether she'd been raped. But she had been strangled, and her wrists and ankles bore the same ligature marks as the other victims. She was 28-year-old, Jane King, a model, and actress. She'd been an attractive and vibrant blonde before the strangler had snuffed out her life.

With the body count mounting, the LAPD, Glendale PD, and L.A. County Sheriff's Department (not always the best of friends) knew they had to work together. A task force comprising 30 officers was established and was soon overwhelmed with tip-offs and suggestions from concerned citizens.

There were no further discoveries over the holiday weekend, but on Tuesday, November 29, the naked body of a young woman was found lying partially in the street in Glendale's Mount Washington area. The ligature marks on her ankles, wrists, and neck, marked her out as a Hillside Strangler victim. There was evidence of torture too, including burn marks on the palms of her hands.

The young victim was identified as Lauren Wagner, an 18-year-old student who lived with her parents in the San Fernando Valley. Lauren's father had woken that morning to find her car parked across the street with the door open. Questioning the neighbors, he'd found that one of them, Beulah Stofer, had witnessed Lauren's abduction, even though she hadn't realized it at the time.

Stofer said that she'd seen Lauren pull up to the curb at around nine o'clock. Two men had pulled their car up beside her, boxing her in. There had been an argument during which Stofer heard Lauren call out, "You won't get away with this!" Then the men had sped off in their car, taking Lauren with them.

Beulah Stofer had gotten a good look at the men and their vehicle. The car was a large sedan, dark in color with a white vinyl top. The men were described as "Latin-looking," one tall and young with acne scars; the other, older and shorter with bushy hair. She was sure that she would be able to identify them again.

The information was valuable, but the murder of Lauren Wagner posed a new problem for investigators. Previously, the killers had confined their murderous activities to Hollywood and Glendale. With this murder, they were spreading their wings. It seems they now regarded the entire city as their hunting ground. Nobody knew where the stranglers would strike next.

With no new leads to follow, detectives looked over the three prostitute murders with which the stranglers had announced their deadly presence. The first to die had been an African-American woman named Yolanda Washington. Her raped and strangled body had been found near the Forest Lawn Cemetery on October 17, 1977.

Two weeks later, the Los Angeles County Sheriff's Department, responded to a report regarding the body of a young woman discovered in La Crescenta, a town just north of Glendale. The victim was a 15-year-old prostitute named Judith Miller. Detectives began questioning pedestrians along her normal beat on Hollywood Boulevard and soon found a man who claimed to have seen Judith getting into a car with two men. He said he'd know them again if he saw them. But the prospects of solving the murder didn't look good. The only other clue was a tiny piece of fluff, found clinging to the victim's eyelid.

Then on November 6, 1977, the body of another strangulation victim turned up in Glendale. She was Lissa Kastin, a 21-year-old waitress who had recently confided in her mother that she was in desperate need of money and might turn to prostitution. She had last been seen leaving the restaurant where she worked, at around 9 o'clock on the night she'd been murdered.

Following that murder had come that horrendous Thanksgiving week, leading to the formation of the Hillside Strangler task force. But the killers then went quiet, perhaps thinking there was too much heat, they lay low for two weeks, re-emerging in mid-December to murder blonde call girl, Kimberly Diane Martin.

Martin had worked for the Climax modeling agency. On the night of her murder, the agency had received a call beckoning her to Apartment 114 at 1950 Tamarind. She'd been found the next day, her body discarded on a steep hillside bordering Alvarado Street.

This time, police had what looked like a couple of good leads. However, neither of these checked out. The killer had called the escort agency from a pay phone at the Hollywood Public Library, and the apartment Kimberly Martin had been called to, did not exist.

No significant progress was made through December and January, but there were no new murders either. Then, on Thursday, February 16, an attractive young woman by the name of Cindy Hudspeth was murdered. Like the other victims, she'd been raped and strangled. Then her body had been placed in the trunk of her car and pushed down a hillside on Angeles Crest. Ligature marks on the neck, wrists and ankles confirmed her as a Hillside Strangler victim.

Police continued working the case. But as the months passed with no new leads, nor any more killings by the Hillside Strangler, the trail began to go cold. The activities of the task force were scaled down. Detectives began working fresher cases.

Almost a year later, police in Bellingham, Washington received a missing persons report on two Western Washington University students, Karen Mandic and Diane Wilder. Officers working the case learned that the girls had accepted a house-sitting job from a friend of theirs, a security guard named Ken Bianchi. However, when officers called on Bianchi, he claimed to know nothing about the arrangement and insisted that he didn't even know the girls. He also offered an alibi for the night the girls went missing. He had been at a Sheriff's Reserve meeting, he said.

Bellingham police chief, Terry Mangan, wasn't happy with the explanation and became even more suspicious when he found that Bianchi hadn't attended the meeting, as he'd claimed. Mangan next visited the girls' apartment and found the address of the Bayside house the two were to house-sit. A look at the security company's records showed that Kenneth Bianchi was responsible for the property. Mangan also saw that Karen Mandic's car was missing and learned that, on the night of her disappearance, Bianchi had used a company truck, supposedly to take it in for repair. Except, he'd never done so.

Concerned now that the girls may have come to harm, Mangan asked the Highway Patrol to check for sites where a car might have been dumped. When that didn't turn up any results, he turned to the media and arranged for them to broadcast photographs of the missing girls and a description of their car.

Shortly thereafter, a woman called in to say that a car had been abandoned in a heavily wooded area near her home. Police rushed to the scene and had their worst fears realized. Inside the vehicle were the bodies of Karen Mandic and Diane Wilder. Both had been strangled.

While the murdered women were being taken to the morgue, Chief Mangan ordered that Kenneth Bianchi be brought in for questioning. Bianchi was quite happy to oblige. The well groomed, six-footer was friendly and articulate. He told officers that he lived with his girlfriend, Kelli Boyd, and their infant son, having moved from L.A. a year ago. Kelli was stunned that someone as gentle-natured as Ken was being questioned about a double homicide. Bianchi's employee, too, had nothing but good things to say about him.

Bellingham police, though, were not taken in. They were convinced that Bianchi knew more than he was saying and were sure that the forensic evidence they'd gathered would implicate him. But they were afraid that Bianchi might flee the jurisdiction if they got too close. What they needed was an excuse to take him into custody and Bianchi made it easy for them. Detectives found stolen items in his house – items he'd pilfered from the homes he was supposed to be protecting.

With Bianchi in custody, Chief Mangan revisited the evidence in the double homicide. Something about the case bothered him and he soon realized what it was. The way the two Bellingham victims had been bound reminded him of the Hillside Strangler murders. It had also not escaped his notice that Bianchi had moved to Washington a year ago, at around the time the Hillside Strangler killings had abruptly stopped. He placed a couple of call to Los Angeles and spoke to Detective Frank Salerno at the L.A. County Sheriff's Office.

Salerno was very interested in the call from Bellingham, even more so once he realized that Bianchi had lived close to three of the L.A. victims. He immediately arranged to head up to

Washington, while other officers worked to uncover Bianchi's activities while he'd lived in L.A. It wasn't long before there was substantial evidence linking Bianchi to the Hillside Strangler murders. Jewelry found in his possession matched distinctive pieces worn by two of the victims, while hair and fiber evidence further corroborated his guilt.

Hoping to glean more information on Kenneth Bianchi, police in L.A. released a photo to the media. Within hours, they got a call from a lawyer named David Wood. Wood said he'd rescued two girls from Bianchi and his cousin, Angelo Buono, who had forced the young women into prostitution. He described Buono as vulgar, brutal and sadistic, with a pathological hatred of woman.

Based on this tip-off, detectives paid Buono a visit and soon decided that he fit the profile. In fact, they were almost certain that this crude, ugly man was the other Hillside Strangler.

Except believing it, and proving it, were two different things and neither Kenneth Bianchi nor Angelo Buono was talking. Bianchi, in fact, was already working on an insanity defense. The idea had probably been planted in his mind by a psychiatric social worker. Having examined Bianchi, the man commented that he couldn't understand how someone so mild-mannered could have strangled two women - unless he was suffering from multiple personality disorder. Bianchi immediately jumped on this idea. He'd recently seen the movie Sybil, about a woman with multiple personalities, and drawing on this he created an alter ego, Steve Walker, who he claimed had committed the murders in L.A. and Washington.

In order to beef up this line of defense, Bianchi's attorney arranged for him to be interviewed by Dr. John G. Watkins, an expert on multiple personalities. Watkins was certain that Bianchi was suffering from the disorder. An independent expert, Dr. Ralph Allison, was also asked to examine Bianchi. He was even more convinced than Watkins that Bianchi's was a genuine case of MPD.

Prosecutors, though, had no intention of letting Bianchi's insanity defense go unchallenged. Dr. Martin Orne, an authority on hypnosis, was called in to assess whether Bianchi was faking or not. Orne had developed procedures to determine whether a subject was actually hypnotized or was just pretending to be. Bianchi's responses convinced Orne that Bianchi was faking.

With his insanity defense blown, the L.A. County District Attorney offered Bianchi a deal - plead guilty and testify against Buono and in exchange prosecutors would not seek the death penalty. They'd also allow him to serve his time in California rather than at Washington's tough Walla Walla prison. Bianchi agreed.

Over the next weeks, he described to investigators how he and Buono had abducted, raped, tortured, and strangled their victims before dumping their bodies. They often posed as policemen to get victims to go with them, he said, then drove them back to Angelo Buono's auto upholstery shop. With neither remorse nor emotion, he described the brutal torture their victims were subjected to – sodomy, electric shocks, gassing, injection with acid-based cleaners, rape with various objects, including soda bottles. The descriptions sickened even hardened detectives. Bianchi seemed unmoved.

Based on his confession, Bianchi received two life sentences in the state of Washington. He was then transferred to California where he was sentenced to additional life terms. Now it was time to bring his brutal cousin, Angelo Buono, to justice.

Buono was arrested on October 22, 1979. Prosecutors believed that it would be a straightforward case. After all, they had Kenneth Bianchi's testimony, as well as physical evidence and eyewitness reports to the various abductions. As it turned out, the case was anything but simple.

First, Bianchi refused to co-operate, claiming amnesia and constantly changing his story. Then, the prosecutor decided that, in view of Bianchi's antics, he wanted to drop the charges against Buono, a move which Judge Ronald George flatly refused. Following the judge's decision, the L.A. District Attorney's office withdrew from the case and a special investigator was appointed.

Finally, in November 1979, the case went ahead, to be immediately bogged down by continuances, motions, and a protracted jury selection process. The first evidence in the case was only presented in the spring of 1982.

When the time arrived for Bianchi to testify, he was in no mood to co-operate. That is until the no-nonsense Judge George stepped in. He informed Bianchi that his lack of cooperation amounted to violating his plea-bargain agreement, which meant that he would be sent to serve his time in the uncompromising environment of Walla Walla. Bianchi quickly fell into line.

On October 21, 1983, after what was, at the time, the longest criminal trial in U.S. history, the matter went to the jury. Ten days later, they delivered a guilty verdict in the murder of Lauren Wagner, and over the following days found Buono guilty of all but the Yolanda Washington murder.

As a convicted multiple murderer, Buono faced either the death penalty or life in prison without the possibility of parole. Yet, despite the sheer depravity of the crimes, the jury inexplicably opted for the latter, clearly annoying the judge, who said as much in his summing up.

Angelo Buono was sent to serve his sentence at Folsom Prison, where he reportedly refused to leave his cell, so afraid was he of being attacked by other inmates. He died of an apparent heart attack on September 21, 2002.

Despite his protestations, Kenneth Bianchi's plea deal was vacated and he was shipped off to Walla Walla. At time of writing, he is still there.

Larry Eyler

The Highway Killer

Bundy, Gacy, Dahmer – infamous names of vicious killers that anyone with even a cursory interest in serial murder will know immediately. Larry Eyler is not as well known. Yet, the so-called, "Highway Killer," was every bit as brutal, as heartless, and as deadly, as the aforementioned three. And he may have claimed more victims than any of them.

For a period of two years, from late 1982 to 1984, the Highway Killer cruised the roads of the American Midwest from Wisconsin to Kansas, picking up hitchhikers and male prostitutes. His attacks were frenzied - hacking and stabbing and then mutilating the bodies before dumping them in rural locations. At least ten victims died at his hands before police realized that they had a serial killer on their hands. Even then, the investigation was hampered by interdepartmental bickering and procedural ineptitude, which allowed the killer to walk free and kill again.

The first Highway Killer victim was discovered on October 23, 1982. Eventually identified as 19-year-old Steven Crockett, the body was found in a cornfield outside Kankakee, Illinois, about 40 miles south of Chicago. A couple of months later, on Christmas Day, a second corpse, that of 25-year-old John R. Johnson, was found in Lowell, Indiana. As with Steve Crockett, Johnson had been stabbed to death, the body severely mutilated.

In the days prior to the FBI's VICAP program, there was no reason or means for police to connect the two murders. But the alarm bells should have been ringing in Indiana with the discovery of two more mutilated corpses on December 28.

Twenty-three-year-old Steven Agan was found near Newport, in Vermillion County. His throat had been slashed, and he'd been so violently stabbed in the abdomen that his intestines had spilled out from the jagged wound. John Roach, a 21-year-old from Indianapolis was dumped along Interstate Highway 70 in Putnam County. Like Agan, he'd been stabbed and severely mutilated.

Because neither Vermillion nor Putnam Counties had their own forensic lab, both victims were transported to Bloomington Hospital. Here, pathologist Dr. John Pless noted a similarity in the stab patterns and alerted investigators to the possibility of a serial killer. Sadly, they chose to ignore his warning, dismissing it as "alarmist."

But while police may have been slow to accept what, in retrospect, seems like an obvious conclusion, members of the Chicago and Indianapolis gay communities were certain that there was a serial killer at work, targeting gay men across the Midwest. In January 1983, a gay newspaper in Indianapolis set up a hotline for members of the public to phone in information on the case. They also ran a series of articles describing the killer as a self-loathing homosexual who killed his sexual partners to refute his own sexuality. A later FBI profile would draw a similar conclusion.

And still the bodies kept showing up. On March 4, 1983, 27-year-old Edgar Underkofler was found stabbed to death outside Danville, Illinois. Two weeks later, Jay Reynolds was found beside U.S. Highway 25 in Fayette County. The 26-year-old had been missing since March 21.

The Highway Killer's seventh victim was 28-year-old Gustavo Herrera, found in Lake County, Illinois, close to the Wisconsin border, on April 8, 1983. He'd been severely mutilated and his right hand had been cut off and was missing from the scene.

One week later, another victim was found, 16-year-old Ervin Gibson, had been stabbed to death and left at Lake Forest, close to I-94. And on May 9, 1983, police were called to the site of yet another mutilated corpse, 18-year-old Jimmy T. Roberts, stabbed more than thirty times, and left in a creek.

There was another discovery on May 9, and this finally, led to police accepting that a serial killer was at work. Twenty-one-year-old Daniel McNeive had been stabbed 27 times, one of the wounds so severe that it left his intestines hanging out of his stomach cavity. As with the Agan and Roach murders, the body was sent to Bloomington Hospital, where Dr. Pless again conducted the autopsy and again declared his suspicions to investigators. This time, they paid attention.

On May 15, 1983, law enforcement officers from several Indiana jurisdictions gathered in Indianapolis to discuss the Highway Murders. As a result of those discussions a task force was set up, under the command of Lieutenant Jerry Campbell, with Sergeant Frank Love assisting. A month later, fifty officers from eight jurisdictions got together to review unsolved cases involving young men stabbed to death and dumped alongside the state's highways.

By this time police had already identified a prime suspect, a 31-year-old resident of Terre Haute by the name of Larry Eyler. Eyler had been brought to the attention of the task force by an anonymous caller, but he was already well known to the police. In August 1978, he'd been involved in a sexually motivated knife attack on a hitchhiker at Terre Haute. Three years later, he'd been arrested for drugging a 14-year-old boy and dumping him in some woods outside of Greencastle, Indiana. Both victims had survived and Eyler had walked when they'd declined to press charges.

With nowhere else to take their investigation, the task force focused all of their attention on Eyler, placing him under constant surveillance. On August 27, they trailed him to an Indianapolis gay bar, watched him leave with another man and followed them to a

Greencastle motel. On this occasion, Eyler's pick-up walked away unharmed, but the Highway Killer would soon strike again.

On August 30, 1983, 28-year-old Ralph Calise left his apartment in Oak Park, Illinois. Calise was in the habit of disappearing for days at a time, so his girlfriend suspected nothing amiss when he didn't return. Three days later, a tree-cutting crew found his mutilated corpse in Lake Forest, close to the sites of the Herrera and Gibson murders. Police found tire tracks and footprints at the scene, the first forensic evidence they'd been able to gather. It was also around this time – September 1983 – that Illinois detectives first learned of Indiana's ongoing investigation into four cases with a startlingly similar pattern.

On September 8, 1983, investigators from Waukegan and Indianapolis met at Crown Point, Indiana to discuss the Highway Murders. Agents from the FBI's Behavioral Science Unit were also present and provided a profile, which was an accurate depiction of Larry Eyler. They described the killer as someone who affected a tough, "macho man" image, who enjoyed wearing military clothing and who hung out at "redneck" bars, all in an effort to deny his sexuality. They described the murders after sex as the "ultimate denial."

On September 30, 1983, Chicago police spotted Larry Eyler cruising an area favored by male prostitutes. The officers took up surveillance and saw Eyler pick up Darl Hayward. Unaware that he was being followed, Eyler began driving south along I-90, forcing Chicago detectives to give up their chase as he crossed into Lake County, Indiana. Amazingly, despite suspecting that a murder was about to be committed, none of the Chicago cops thought to alert their Indiana counterparts.

East of Lowell, Eyler stopped at the side of the highway and persuaded Hayward to walk with him across a field, in order to have sex in an abandoned barn. While they were away, State Trooper Kenneth Buehrle drove by and spotted Eyler's pick-up, parked illegally, and the two men just coming out of the woods.

Buehrle asked Eyler for his driver's license and radioed in to check for outstanding warrants. He had no idea who Eyler was, but members of the Highway Killer task team picked up the broadcast and immediately rushed to the scene.

Eyler was taken to the Lowell barracks, where he surrendered his boots for examination and consented to a search of his truck. That search turned up a bloodstained knife, but as police had no evidence that a crime had been committed, they were forced to let Eyler go.

The next morning, a squad led by Lt. Jerry Campbell raided the Terre Haute home that Eyler shared with University of Indiana professor Robert Little. They removed various items and also phone records on which they found a number of mysterious late-night phone calls, one of them to a man named John Dobrovolskis. Detectives traced Dobrovolskis' home address and found Eyler there. They decided to take Eyler in for questioning, even though they assured him that he wasn't under arrest.

Shortly after Eyler's release, a dismembered torso was found in a plastic trash bag, near Highway 31, in Kenosha County, Wisconsin. The victim would later be identified as Eric Hansen, an 18-year-old male prostitute from St. Francis, Wisconsin.

Then, on October 15, the skeletal remains of an unknown victim were found in Jasper County, Indiana, the bones notched by knife wounds, indicating death by stabbing. Just days later, mushroom hunters found four decomposing bodies on a farm outside Lake Village, Indiana. Two of the victims would never be identified; the other two were 22-year-old Michael Bauer and 19-year-old John Bartlett.

In the meanwhile, investigators were gathering and collating evidence against Eyler. They had human blood on the knife taken from his truck, distinctive nicks on the soles of his boots that matched footprints found at the Calise murder scene, and type A-positive blood (Calise's type) found on the inner lining of his boots. They had the handcuffs seized from Robert Little's home, which were found to be consistent with marks left on Calise's wrists. Likewise, the tire tracks from Eyler's truck matched tracks found at the scene.

Strong as this evidence appeared, prosecutors were to receive a rude shock when they brought it to court. Eyler's attorney, David Schippers, argued that the evidence had been obtained illegally since the search had been carried out after Eyler was arrested on a parking violation, a minor infraction that did not constitute just cause. The judge agreed. The state's entire forensic case, with the exception of the tire track evidence, was disallowed.

On February 2, 1984, Larry Eyler walked from the court a free man. He immediately left Indiana and moved to Chicago, leaving the police to wonder whether he'd just gotten away with multiple murder.

And Eyler might well have escaped justice in the Highway Killer murders were it not for his own arrogance in committing a crime so reckless, so blatant, that it was almost as though he was asking to be caught.

On August 21, 1984, the janitor of an apartment building on West Sherman Street, Chicago, found a number of plastic trash bags overflowing from a dumpster. He began moving them, but as he lifted one of the bags, it split open, disgorging a severed human leg.

The police were called and discovered the dismembered remains of a white male, cut into eight pieces, and split among various bags. Witnesses described seeing a tenant from the building next door throwing the bags into the dumpster. Officers went to question the man. It was Larry Eyler.

Eyler was taken into custody while the police searched his apartment. There, they found a number of bloody hacksaw blades, numerous bloodstains, trash bags matching those the body had been placed in, and a t-shirt belonging to the victim, 16-year-old Danny Bridges.

On September 13, with prosecutors announcing that they intended seeking the death penalty, Larry Eyler entered a not guilty plea. After that, legal maneuvering delayed his trial for nearly two years, meaning the matter was finally heard on July 1, 1986. Then, the jury had little hesitation in convicting Eyler of all counts. On October 3, 1986, Judge Urso sentenced Eyler to death for the murder of Danny Bridges.

Thus began the appeals process, a legal marathon that often sees an inmate spending years, even decades, on death row. While these appeals were ongoing, Eyler was contacted by several Indiana jurisdictions, offering 60-year prison terms in exchange for clearing up unsolved homicides. Eyler agreed, saying that he could provide details of over 20 murders, but only if his death sentence was commuted to life in prison. Cook County prosecutors flatly rejected such a deal.

Larry Eyler, however, would never make it to the electric chair. He died of AIDS on March 6, 1994. He was 41 years old.

Donald 'Pee Wee' Gaskins

The Meanest Man in America

"I have walked the same path as God. By taking lives and making others afraid, I became God's equal." - Pee Wee Gaskins

Donald Gaskins was born on March 13, 1933, in Florence County, South Carolina. He never knew his father, who hit the road long before Donald was born. Instead, the young boy was raised by a succession of his mother's brutal boyfriends. When she eventually married one of them in 1943, Donald acquired not only a stepfather but four stepsiblings as well. But the new man was no better than his predecessors, and Pee Wee (so called because of his diminutive size) received regular beatings, something he came to regard as normal.

Pee Wee was good with his hands, but a poor student. In 1944, at the age of just 11, he quit school to work on cars at a local garage. At the same time, he teamed up with two young delinquents named Danny and Marsh, to form a marauding gang they dubbed "The Trouble Trio." Starting off with petty thefts, they soon graduated to burglaries, and more serious crimes, eventually building up enough capital from their criminal activities to buy an old car. This allowed them to range further afield and by their early teens they were visiting prostitutes and committing rapes, including those of young boys. However, the trio eventually pushed their luck too far. After they gang-raped Marsh's younger sister, Danny and Marsh were hauled in by their parents and beaten bloody with a leather strap. Gaskins escaped only because his stepfather defended him with a shotgun.

As soon as they recovered, Pee Wee's cohorts fled the jurisdiction, and Pee Wee started working alone, burglarizing houses in the region. Inevitably, though, he ran out of luck. Accosted by a young girl at one of his robberies, Gaskins buried a hatchet in her skull. He thought she was dead, but the girl survived to identify him and he found himself shipped to the South Carolina Industrial School for Boys.

Gaskins would later say that he received his "real education" at the state reformatory. On his second night, he was attacked in the shower, beaten and gang-raped by a group of 20 boys. Afterward, he accepted protection from the dormitory "Boss Boy," in exchange for sexual favors. Gaskins would attempt three escapes from the reformatory, but he was captured and returned each time, suffering beatings, solitary confinement, and hard labor for his trouble. Eventually, in 1950, with less than a year of his sentence to run, he made good his escape.

Pee Wee fled to Sumter, where he joined a traveling carnival, and soon after married the first of his six wives, a 13-year-old member of the crew. His new bride convinced him to return to the reformatory and he did, fulfilling the last three months of his sentence in solitary confinement.

Released on his 18th birthday, Gaskins got a job working on a tobacco plantation. But criminality never strayed far from Pee Wee Gaskins. Soon he had teamed up with another ex-reformatory inmate and was committing theft and arson (often in cahoots with the landowners, as part of an insurance fraud).

Eventually, after they'd torched half-a-dozen barns, stories of their activities began to circulate. When his employer's teenage daughter taunted him about the rumors, Gaskins snapped, picked up a hammer and cracked the girl's skull. Arrested soon after for arson, assault, and attempted murder, Gaskins struck a deal and pled guilty. Unfortunately for him, the judge decided not to honor the prosecutor's promise of 18 months. He sentenced Gaskins to five-years, then added another year for contempt after Gaskins cursed him.

Gaskins entered the South Carolina state prison in the fall of 1952, and he soon realized that it was a big step up from the reformatory. Instead of "Boss Boys," there were "Power Men." In order to avoid the gang rapes and beatings he'd suffered before, Pee Wee decided that he'd have to become a Power Man himself.

The thing was, Pee Wee was only 5-foot-four. If he wanted to make a name for himself, he'd have to do something that laid down a marker, something that made a statement.

He decided on murder and began looking for the biggest, meanest, victim he could find. Eventually, he decided on a con he picked named Hazel Brazell, who was so vicious that not even the guards dared call him by his despised first name.

Gaskins began to ingratiate himself with Brazell, bringing him gifts of food from the kitchen, and hanging around his cell. Eventually, he saw his chance. Finding Brazell on the toilet, Gaskins cut his throat, then waited calmly for the guards to arrive, while his victim lay convulsing and bleeding to death on the floor. He claimed self-defense and pled to manslaughter, adding an extra nine years to his sentence. It was worth it, though. No one messed with Pee Wee Gaskins after that.

In 1955, Gaskins hatched a plot to escape from prison in a garbage truck. Stealing a car, he worked his way back to Florida, then to Cookville, Tennessee, where he was arrested for trying to help a prisoner escape. He was returned to the Palmetto State Prison, his little escapade having earned him an additional three years for driving a stolen car across state lines.

Gaskins was eventually paroled in August 1961, and soon thereafter landed a job as a driver for a traveling preacher named George Todd. Not that any of the biblical lessons washed off on Pee Wee. He used the opportunity to commit burglary, and other crimes, wherever they traveled. During his second year driving for

Reverend Todd, Gaskins was arrested for the statutory rape of a 12-year-old girl in Florence County. He escaped from the courthouse while awaiting his arraignment and fled to Greensboro, North Carolina.

But his freedom was short-lived. Arrested and sentenced to six years on the statutory rape charge, he was returned to the state pen in Columbia, where his reputation as a 'Power Man' remained intact. No one bothered him and he did easy time until his parole in November 1968.

Gaskins' next move was back to Sumter, South Carolina, where he got a job working construction. In his spare time, he stripped down stolen cars and cruised the bars for sex. But he still raged and brooded over all the women who had rejected him. It brought about what he'd later refer to as "aggravated and bothersome feelings." He suffered from headaches and stomach cramps, and to alleviate them he started taking long drives along the Carolina coast. It was on one of these drives, in September 1969, that stopped for a hitchhiker.

The girl was young and blond and pretty. Gaskins picked her up at Myrtle Beach and she said that she was on her way to Charleston. Almost immediately, he began propositioning her. When she laughed him off, he knocked her unconscious and drove to an old logging road. After he raped and sodomized the girl, he spent some time torturing and mutilating her with a knife. She was still alive when he dropped her weighted body into a swamp.

Gaskins later called that first murder "a miracle, a beam of light, a vision." From then on, he trolled the coastal highways on weekends, looking for victims. He even came up with a name for his new hobby. He called the murders, "Coastal Kills," committed for no other reason than to amuse himself. And he began refining his methods. Eventually, he could keep his victims alive and screaming for hours, sometimes for days.

By 1970, Gaskins was averaging one "Coastal Kill" every six weeks. He began experimenting with different torture methods, getting ideas by browsing hardware stores and observing the tools on display. He was always disappointed when his victims died too quickly. "I preferred for them to last as long as possible," he later wrote. In 1972, he committed his first double homicide, killing two girls that he picked up together. And in March 1974, he claimed his first male victims. Gaskins said he picked up the two longhaired boys thinking they were girls but decided to kill them anyway. He drove them both to a hideout near Charleston, where he sodomized and tortured them, then cooked and ate their severed genitals while they were still alive.

Gaskins lost track of the victims he murdered for fun between September 1969 and December 1975. They became just a "jumble of faces and bodies," to him, but by his own estimation, he killed between 80 and 90. Sadistic murder was addictive. "I finally reached the point where I wanted the bothersomeness to start," he recalled. "I looked forward to it every month, because it felt so good relieving myself of it."

The "Coastal Kills," were recreational to him, but from 1970, Gaskins began committing what he called his, "Serious Murders."

That is, he began killing people he knew, usually for profit or to hide evidence of other criminal acts.

His first two "serious" victims were his 15-year-old niece, Janice Kirby, and her 17-year-old friend, Patricia Alsobrook. Gaskins had been planning to rape Janice for some time, and in November 1970, he finally saw an opportunity. The girls were out drinking, and Gaskins offered them a ride home. Instead, he took them to an abandoned house where he ordered them to take their clothes off. When they resisted, he pulled a gun and overpowered them, before beating them unconscious. After raping both of the girls, he drowned them in a water barrel and then buried them in separate locations. Gaskins was questioned about the girls' disappearances but said they'd been alive and unharmed when he'd dropped them off. Without evidence to the contrary, the police had to let it drop.

A month later, Gaskins kidnapped, raped and murdered Peggy Cuttino, the 12-year-old daughter of South Carolina senator James Cuttino, Jr. Then, shortly after he married his pregnant girlfriend on January 1, 1971, he murdered 20-year-old Martha Dicks, an African American woman who apparently became infatuated with him.

In late 1971, Gaskins moved to Charleston with his wife and child. A year later, he killed Eddie Brown and his wife Bertie. Brown was a gunrunner who Gaskins believed was trying to set him up. In July 1973, he moved to Prospect, South Carolina, where he committed three more murders, including that of a 14-year-old runaway, Jackie Freeman, who he claims to have tortured and cannibalized.

Heinous as the Freeman murder was, the next one was almost beyond evil. Gaskins offered a ride to 23-year-old Doreen Dempsey and her two-year-old daughter Robin Michelle. He promised to take them to the bus station but instead drove into the woods, where he killed Doreen with a hammer, then raped and sodomized the child before strangling her to death.

Gaskins next "serious murder" was the 1974 killing of Johnny Sellars, a car thief who owed him $1,000. Gaskins got tired of waiting for the money, so he shot Sellars, then stabbed his girlfriend, Jessie Ruth Judy, to death so that she couldn't report Sellars missing. He followed that up by killing Horace Jones, after the man made a pass at Gaskins' wife.

Writing from prison, Gaskins would later recall 1975 as "my killingest year." He started it off by killing a man and two women, "hippie types," as he described them. Their van had broken down near Georgetown and he offered them a lift to the nearest garage. Instead, he took them to a nearby swamp where he handcuffed and tortured them before killing them by drowning. Gaskins used an accomplice in disposing of the van, an ex-con named Walter Neely. He'd later have cause to regret that decision.

The next murder Gaskins carried out was the contract killing of Silas Yates, a wealthy Florence County farmer. Gaskins was paid $1,500 for the job by Suzanne Kipper, Yates one-time lover who was furious when he ended their relationship. Later, he'd use his knowledge of the murder to extort sex from Kipper on demand.

A while later, Diane Neely (sister of Walter) tried to blackmail Gaskins over the murder. Bad mistake. Gaskins lured Neely and her lover, Avery Howard, to a wooded area where he shot them both and interred them in a shallow grave.

Next, he murdered Kim Ghelkins, a 13-year-old who angered him by rejecting his sexual advances. Gaskins reacted in typical fashion by raping, torturing and strangling the girl, then burying her in the woods. Not long after, he killed 25-year-old Dennis Bellamy and 15-year-old Johnny Knight. The pair had tried to burgle Pee Wee's workshop. He shot them both and buried their bodies, once again enlisting the help of Walter Neely.

But the net was finally beginning to close in on Gaskins. In October 1975, Sumter deputies, investigating the murder of Kim Ghelkins, searched his home and found some of Kim's clothes. Charged with contributing to the delinquency of a minor, Gaskins tried to flee to Georgia, but was apprehended at the bus station. Then, while Gaskins was in jail awaiting trial, the world came crashing down around him. Walter Neely cracked under interrogation and confessed everything, leading investigators to the various spots where Gaskins had buried his victims. In short order, they found the remains of Bellamy, Knight, Sellars, Judy, Howard, Diane Neely, Doreen Dempsey and her daughter Robin Michelle.

Gaskins went on trial on May 24, 1976, and despite his protestations of innocence, he was found guilty and sentenced to die in the electric chair. But Gaskins would spend just six months on death row. In November 1976, the U.S. Supreme Court vacated all death sentences commuting them to life imprisonment.

Donald Gaskins had been spared from the executioner. But he wasn't done killing yet. By 1982, he was something of a minor celebrity in the South Carolina prison system and his mechanical skills had earned him a job as a maintenance trustee.

Incarcerated on death row at the time was an inmate named Rudolph Tyner, sentenced to die for killing an elderly couple named Bill and Myrtle Moon during a bungled robbery. Except Myrtle Moon's son, Tony Cimo, wasn't about to see his mother's killer sitting on death row for 20 years while the legal system cycled through appeal after appeal. He wanted Tyner dead now and, through prison contacts, he hired Pee Wee Gaskins to do the job.

Gaskins decided that poison was the best way to go. He started by befriending Tyner and winning his trust by supplying him with food, marijuana, and pills. Once he had Tyner on the hook, he passed him a box of candy laced with poison "strong enough to kill a horse." It didn't work. And neither did five subsequent attempts over the next 12 months. Despite an ever-increasing dosage, Tyner merely suffered stomach cramps.

Eventually, Gaskins gave up on poison and decided to use explosives instead. Cimo smuggled in wiring, hardware and plastic explosive, which Gaskins placed in a homemade intercom. He told Tyner that the device would allow them to communicate between their cells. On September 2, 1982, he arranged a test run. When Tyner placed his head to the set, Gaskins pressed a button, blowing him to smithereens. "The last thing he heard was me laughing," Gaskins said.

Ironically, the state of South Carolina, which had previously tried, and failed, to execute Donald Gaskins, now had him for killing a man who was destined to die anyway. Gaskins was tried, found guilty of murder and sentenced to death. He went to the electric chair on September 6, 1991.

H.H. Holmes

The Torture Doctor

"I was born with the evil one standing as my sponsor beside the bed where I was ushered into the world, and he has been with me since." - H. H. Holmes

H.H. Holmes is sometimes called America's first serial killer, and while that title is inaccurate (the Harpe brothers, for example, preceded him), he is certainly the first to have become a media sensation. It is easy to see why. Holmes was no ordinary criminal. He was a man born to the dark arts. A swindler, a thief, a bigamist, a glib seducer of young women, and lest we forget, a torturer and mass murderer of quite monstrous proportions. By the time he went to the gallows at age 35, Holmes had admitted to 27 murders, although most commentators believe that was well shy of the mark. Many of these murders had been committed at his labyrinthine 'Murder Castle' in Chicago, a building constructed for no other purpose that to lure the unwary traveler to a horrific death. But we're getting ahead of ourselves. Let's start at the beginning.

Holmes was born Herman Webster Mudgett in Gilmanton Academy, New Hampshire in 1861. He was an intelligent child, though considered by his classmates to be slightly odd, which made him an easy target for bullies. At home, too, young Herman got his fair share of lickings. His father was a devout Methodist who believed staunchly in the proverb, "Spare the rod and spoil the child."

Two incidents from Mudgett's childhood stand out to provide clues as to the man he would become. The first was the tragic death of his one and only friend, who suffered a fatal fall while exploring an abandoned house with Mudgett. There were suggestions that the boy might have been pushed (with Mudgett the obvious perpetrator) but without proof, the matter went no further. The other was a bullying incident, where a couple of the village toughs terrorized Mudgett with a skeleton stolen from the local doctor's surgery. Mudgett would later claim that this incident sparked his lifelong interest in anatomy. By age eleven, he was dissecting frogs and salamanders. Later, he'd graduate to stray dogs and cats.

Mudgett finished high school in 1877, at age 16. Thereafter, he took teaching jobs in Gilmanton and later in Alton, New Hampshire. And it was in Alton that he met Clara Lovering, who later became his wife and the mother of his two children. Clara was from a wealthy family, and when Mudgett expressed an interest in studying medicine, they agreed to sponsor him. He enrolled at the University of Michigan, Ann Arbor in 1882, emerging four years later with a medical degree.

But Mudgett had no real interest in practicing medicine. While enrolled at UM, he had already perpetrated a number of profitable scams involving cadavers stolen from the university's dissection lab. In what was to become an established M.O., he'd take out an insurance policy on a fictitious person, then acquire a corpse, disfigure it, and claim that it was the insured person who had died in an accident.

Mudgett ranged far and wide carrying out his scams and inevitably his marriage to Clara suffered. Eventually, he abandoned his wife and family altogether and began wandering the northeast, committing fraud after fraud. He was also linked, during this time, with the disappearances of two young boys, in Mooers Forks, New York, and in Philadelphia. On each occasion, Mudgett fled town before the police got around to questioning him. Eventually, he ended up in Chicago. It was there that he first began using his infamous alias, H.H. Holmes.

Holmes arrived in Chicago in August 1886, just as that city was preparing to host the World's Fair, a massive exposition that would run for six months and attract over 27 million people. His first step was to apply for the position of prescription clerk at a pharmacy on 63rd and South Wallace Streets. The business was run by a Mrs. Holton, but she disappeared, along with a daughter, shortly after Holmes started working there. Thereafter, he answered queries as to the whereabouts of the Holtons by saying that they had moved to California after selling the store to him. Neither woman was ever heard from again.

Now in control of the business, Holmes used his newly acquired equity to buy a vacant lot, directly across the road. There he began work on a massive building, three stories high and taking up an entire block. He called it the World's Fair Hotel, although it was known locally as "The Castle" due to its vast size. The ground floor was taken up by commercial space that accommodated various shops (including Holmes' relocated pharmacy). The upper floor was given to small rooms which Holmes planned on renting to visitors to the World's Fair.

But it was the middle floor and the basement that were the most peculiar. Here, there were soundproofed rooms with peepholes, asbestos-padded walls, gas pipes, and vents that Holmes could control from his quarters. Some of the rooms had low ceilings and trapdoors. There were secret passages, false floors, and a room that contained torture equipment. There was even a specially equipped surgery. Some rooms had greased chutes that emptied into the basement. Within the basement itself was a massive furnace and an asbestos-lined pit with gas jets to either side. There was also an "elasticity determinator," basically an elongated bed with straps, designed to see how far the human body could be stretched. Finally, there were several large vats, filled with acid.

One can only imagine why Holmes would have had all of these bizarre features incorporated into his home. Suffice to say that he had gone to considerable lengths to keep them a secret. During construction of the Castle, he had constantly hired and fired different work crews. He, and he alone, knew the layout of the building and its unsettling fixtures.

An untold number of people, most of them women, entered the Castle but never left. Many of these were young employees at the only legitimate enterprise Holmes ever operated, a copier business. Others were hotel guests and Holmes' numerous lovers and their children.

What became of them? We know the answer to that question only because of Holmes' later confession. Some were locked in soundproof rooms and then gassed to death while Holmes watched through a peephole. Others were hanged in a room that Holmes called his "secret hanging chamber." Still others were asphyxiated inside a huge bank vault. There was also a soundproof room that could only be entered through a trapdoor in the ceiling. Holmes would lock his victims in here and leave them to die of hunger and thirst. The victims' bodies were then transferred to the basement via one of the chutes. There, they'd be either burned or dissolved in acid. Some were sold as cadavers or were stripped of flesh with the skeletons sold to medical schools. Others were stretched on Holmes' rack until flesh and bone were torn asunder. This was of particular fascination to Holmes, who believed that the human body could be elongated to create a race of giants.

Many of Holmes' victims will forever remain nameless. They were simply unfortunate young women who had come from all over America to visit the World's Fair and who were never seen again. But we do know the names of some of those who were unlucky enough to fall into Dr. Holmes' clutches.

Julia Conner was an attractive blonde who was married to one of Holmes' pharmacy employees, Ned Conner. Holmes had decided to seduce Julia almost as soon as he set eyes on her and to this extent had offered Conner and his family free board at the Castle. Soon after, he and Julia were lovers. When Conner found out about the affair, he quit his job and moved out, leaving his wife and daughter behind. All went well until 1891 when Julia fell pregnant and demanded that Holmes marry her. It was a bad mistake. Holmes agreed to marriage but only on condition that Julia had an abortion, which he would perform himself. On the operating table in his surgery, he murdered Julia by overdosing her with chloroform. Later, he also killed her little girl.

Another woman to fall prey to Holmes was a young heiress from Fort Worth, Texas named Minnie Williams. Holmes had met Minnie while on a business trip to Boston and she quickly fell for his glib line of talk. After she returned to Texas, he kept up a correspondence with her. Eventually, in April 1893, he persuaded her to join him in Chicago. Shortly thereafter, Minnie signed over the deeds of her Fort Worth property to a certain Alexander Bond (one of the many aliases used by Holmes). Holmes then encouraged Minnie to invite her sister Annie to join her in Chicago. Within a week of Annie's arrival, Holmes had seduced her too, but things got rapidly more complicated after that. The sisters quarreled over Holmes affections and he decided to clear the decks. First Annie was gassed to death inside his bank vault. Then Minnie disappeared. (Holmes later maintained that she had moved to England but no trace of her was ever found.)

Aside from his forays into wholesale slaughter, Holmes seemed to derive genuine pleasure out of defrauding people. His latest scheme was to buy furniture and fixtures on credit, sell them off, and then default on his debt. He'd then use any number of devious means to evade his creditors, keeping them at bay for years with false promises and hard luck stories. But by the conclusion of the

World's Fair, Holmes' creditors were fighting back, joining forces to extract payment from the elusive doctor.

Faced with the prospect of court action, Holmes decided that it was time to move on. He abandoned his 'Castle' and fled to Fort Worth and the property he'd stolen from Minnie Williams. There, he began another building project along the lines of his Chicago operation. However, he soon abandoned the idea and hit the road, traveling throughout the United States and Canada, committing frauds wherever he landed. It was during this time that he committed the murder that would lead to his eventual downfall.

In July 1894, Holmes was arrested and briefly incarcerated in St. Louis. While in jail, he struck up a conversation with a train robber named Marion Hedgepeth, who was serving a 25-year sentence. Holmes told his new acquaintance about a plan to defraud an insurance company out of $10,000. However, he needed a lawyer who he could trust with the scheme and offered Hedgepeth $500 if he could recommend one. As it turned out, Hedgepeth knew just the man for the job, a young attorney named Jeptha Howe. After Holmes was released, he sought Howe out.

Holmes' plan was simple and was one he'd pulled many times before. An associate of his named Benjamin Pitezel would be insured under an alias. Then he and Holmes would fake an accident, substituting a cadaver for Pitezel. Holmes attorney would then lodge a claim with the insurance company and the parties would split the loot.

Pitezel duly hired premises in Philadelphia and set himself up as an inventor, under the name B.F. Perry. Not long after, there was a lab explosion that killed and badly disfigured 'Perry,' leaving Holmes free to claim on his insurance policy. But Pitezel had been duped. Holmes had never had any intention of using a substitute body. Instead, he'd knocked Pitezel unconscious, killed him with chloroform and then doused his corpse with benzene before setting it alight. Holmes himself tearfully identified the body of his 'dear friend.' A short while after, he pocketed his $10,000 bounty and disappeared.

Now followed one of the strangest episodes in the whole Holmes' saga. For some reason, Holmes persuaded Pitezel's wife into releasing three of her five children, Alice, Nellie, and Howard, into his custody. He then spent weeks traveling with the children throughout the eastern and northern United States and into Canada, while also moving Mrs. Pitezel along a parallel route, that kept her away from her children. At the same time, he was tagging his latest lover, Georgie Anna Yoke, along. There were times that Mrs. Pitezel, Georgie Anna, and the children, were mere blocks from each other without ever knowing it. Holmes also kept up the pretense to Mrs. Pitezel that her husband was still alive and in hiding.

Why Holmes carried out this bizarre ruse, we shall never know. But somewhere along the way, he must have tired of it, because he started disposing of the children. Howard Pitezel was murdered in the small town of Irvington, Indiana, his body incinerated in a coal stove and the charred remains hidden in a chimney. Alice and Nellie met their end in Toronto, Canada, after Holmes persuaded them to hide in a trunk so that they could jump out to surprise their mother (who Holmes said was due to arrive at any moment).

Once they were inside, he latched the trunk and then fed a hose through a hole he'd drilled for that purpose. The girls were gassed to death and then buried in the cellar where their decomposing bodies would later be found by Frank Geyer, a Philadelphia detective who had been sent to hunt down Holmes.

In the meanwhile, Marion Hedgepeth had been stewing in his jail cell over the $500 Holmes had promised him but had neglected to pay. Angered by the betrayal, he eventually decided to inform on his conniving accomplice. It was his tip-off to police that led to Holmes' eventual arrest in Boston on November 17, 1894, just as he was about to board a steamer ship for England.

With Holmes now in custody, the police began searching the Castle, uncovering evidence of wholesale slaughter. There were items of women's clothing, pieces of jewelry, human hair and several charred human bones. Dried blood caked Holmes' dissection table and there were several scratches on the inside of his bank vault, apparently made by someone who was trying desperately to escape. Investigators dug up the lime pits and found more bones and human hair. Some of the bones were determined to be from a child aged 6 to 8 years. All in all, there was evidence of at least nine murders, although based on missing persons' reports and the evidence of Holmes' neighbors and employees, the police believed that as many as 200 might have been murdered inside the Castle.

None of this evidence, however, would ever be heard in a courtroom. Languishing in Philadelphia's Moyamensing Prison, Holmes was charged with only one murder, that of Benjamin Pitezel.

In the interim, the media had picked up the story and had begun trumpeting lurid headlines about Holmes and his "chamber of horrors." Holmes reaction was typical of the self-absorbed psychopath that he was. He penned a response titled "Holmes' Own Story, in which the Alleged Multi-Murderer and Arch Conspirator Tells of the Twenty-two Tragic Deaths and Disappearances in which he is Said to be Implicated."

The book tells Holmes' story from his childhood and upbringing up until his arrest. In it, he readily admitted to fraud but denied murder, coming up with a plethora of blatantly self-serving explanations for the murders and disappearances attributed to him. Nobody took it seriously, least of all prosecutors. Holmes went on trial for murder on October 28.

The trial lasted five days, with Holmes becoming the first accused murderer in U.S. history to conduct his own defense. However, despite a bright start, Holmes made very little headway in casting doubt on the accusations against him and his lack of emotion over the death of Benjamin Pitezel (a man he described as a friend) hurt his case with the jury. On day two, he asked for his counsel to re-enter the case. By then, the damage was done.

In the end, the jury convicted Holmes of Benjamin Pitezel's murder and the judge sentenced him to death by hanging.

After his request for a new trial failed, Holmes decided to make a full confession (due, in the main, to a $10,000 payment from the Hearst newspaper syndicate). He originally laid claim to killing more than 100 people, then reduced that number to 27, including Benjamin Pitezel and the Pitezel children.

H. H. Holmes was hanged at Moyamensing Prison on May 7, 1896. His death was not an easy one. The hangman had measured the rope too short and, as a result, Holmes did not die instantly, as is common in judicial executions. Instead, he thrashed around at the end of the rope and was slowly asphyxiated, taking a full 15 minutes to die.

Patrick Kearney

The Trash Bag Killer

"Murder excited me and gave me a feeling of dominance." - Patrick Kearney

The Seventies were a tumultuous decade in American history. After the summer of love in 1969, a new and more tolerant era beckoned. The whole country seemed to be in motion and many young people were drawn to California, attracted by its great weather, carefree lifestyle, and permissive attitudes.

Hitchhiking was a popular mode of transport for these young travelers and, in the main, those who stuck out their thumb and headed west, arrived safely. Others though, were not so lucky. During that time, a number of prolific serial killers prowled the highways and byways of southern California - men like Randy Kraft, William Bonin, and Patrick Kearney.

Patrick Wayne Kearney was born in East Los Angeles in 1940, the youngest of three sons. His childhood appears to have been relatively stable, at least as far as his home life was concerned. At school, though, he was an easy target for bullies, a thin, sickly and diminutive child who was painfully shy.

Like many children set upon by their peers, Patrick retreated into his own world, although where other kids might lose themselves in books or games, Kearney (according to his later confession) began developing violent revenge fantasies. By age eight, he said, he knew that he was going to kill people; by his mid-teens, his fantasies had developed into keenly detailed visions of murder; by his mid-twenties, those fantasies had been transformed into reality.

Yet, nothing in Patrick Kearney's life suggested that he might become a serial killer. He was an intelligent boy, who did well at school. After graduating, he served in the military, married, and moved with his wife to Texas. Then, after his marriage failed, he met and fell in love with David Douglas Hill, a 6'2" high school dropout from Lubbock, Texas.

Like Kearney, Hill had spent time in the Army, but he'd been discharged after being diagnosed with an unspecified personality disorder. He'd returned to his hometown and married his high school sweetheart. Then he'd met Patrick Kearney and, not long after, he'd divorced his wife and moved with Kearney to California.

In 1967, the pair set up house together, Kearney finding a job as an aeronautics engineer with the Hughes Aircraft Corporation, Hill staying home and looking after domestic affairs. Their relationship, which would last ten years, was often stormy. Hill would often leave in a huff and spend the night with friends or pick up a one-night stand out of revenge. Occasionally, he even went back home to Lubbock, remaining there for days at a time.

It was on these occasions, with Hill out of the picture, that Kearney's repressed rage would simmer to the surface. That was when he'd hit the streets, cruising the interstate or trawling gay bars, picking out victims who often reminded him of those who had bullied him during his childhood.

Kearney's M.O. was simple, efficient, and consistent. He was primarily a necrophile, meaning he had no interest in keeping his victim alive for torture or any other purpose (unlike his contemporaries Kraft and Bonin). Also, he was a slight man, just 5'5" tall, unable to physically subdue victims who tended to be bigger and physically stronger than him. The method he developed compensated for both these factors.

After picking up a man, Kearney would typically shoot him in the head with his Derringer .22. He'd do this while still driving the car in order to catch his victim by surprise. He became particularly adept at steering the vehicle with his left hand while firing with his right. With the victim now under his control, Kearney would drive to a secluded spot where he'd have sex with the corpse. Then he'd dismember the body with a hacksaw, place the sections in trash bags and dispose of them at various locations along the freeways, or out in the desert, where coyotes and insects would consume the remains.

On the occasions that he killed people in his own home, he would dissect the body in the bathtub, drain it of blood and wash the body parts carefully. Then he'd pack the pieces in bags secured with duct tape. He was very careful not to leave any trace evidence, something he'd learned by studying various books on serial killers.

How many men did Kearney kill in this way? He was charged with 21 murders and confessed to 35. Investigators who worked the case believe that the number could be as high as 43. And there were child victims too, among them eight-year-old Merle Chance, and Ronald Dean Smith, aged just 5.

Kearney committed his first murder in 1968 while living in Culver City, California, with David Hill. During one of Hill's absences, Kearney picked up a man he knew only as "George." He brought George back to his apartment, shooting him almost immediately after they entered. Then, he dragged the body to the bathroom and dismembered it with an X-Acto knife. Kearney then extracted the bullet from the head so that it couldn't be traced to his gun. Later, he buried the remains behind his garage and didn't kill again for a year, fearful that he'd be caught.

He wasn't, of course, and eventually he returned to stalking the freeways and bars of southern California, in his VW Bug or in his truck, sometimes taking a victim a month. "It was easy," he said, "easy to pick them up, easy to kill them, and easy to get rid of the bodies."

The Trash Bag Murders first came to the attention of police on April 13, 1975, when the body of Albert Rivera, 21, was found packed in a heavy-duty trash bag, near Highway 74, east of San Juan Capistrano. Soon police were inundated with gruesome new discoveries, each of them bearing the killer's unique signature, bodies neatly dismembered and packaged, none of them bearing any viable clues. The killer was elusive, the case complicated by other serial killers working the same turf at the time. It seemed that police were never going to catch a break in the case.

But then, they did catch a break. On Sunday, March 13, 1977, 17-year-old John LaMay disappeared.

LaMay had told a neighbor that he was going to Redondo Beach to see a guy by the name of Dave, who he'd met at a gym in downtown L.A. When he didn't come home that night, or the following day, his frantic mother called the police, certain that something had happened to him. The police were less concerned. John LaMay was probably out partying with friends. They dealt with calls like this all the time.

Except LaMay wasn't out partying. He'd gone to the address that David Hill had given him, only to find that Hill wasn't home. Hill's roommate was though, and he told LaMay to come inside, to wait for Dave's return. Once inside Kearney invited the young man to watch TV, then snuck up behind him and shot him in the back of the head (on a whim, he'd later tell police). Kearney then cut up the body, packaged it, and disposed of it along the highway.

John LaMay's remains were discovered five days later, on March 18, beside a stretch of road near Corona. He had been dismembered, the body parts washed and drained of blood, and then packed neatly into five trash bags. The bags had been sealed with nylon filament tape and crammed into an empty 80-gallon oil drum. The head was missing, but a distinctive birthmark clearly identified the victim.

Police returned to John LaMay's home and questioned his neighbors, one of whom told the story of LaMay going to visit someone named Dave in Redondo Beach. That combination of the name Dave and the location (Redondo Beach) struck a chord with one of the investigators. Then it came to him, he'd recently called at the home of David Hill during routine questioning about the disappearance of 8-year-old Merle Chance.

When the police called on the Kearney/Hill residence again, Patrick Kearney welcomed them in, expressed his concern for the missing teen, and assured police that he hadn't seen the boy. He seemed genuine enough, but detectives were not here merely to question him. The killer of John LaMay had slipped up, leaving a few carpet fibers caught in the duct tape that secured the plastic bags. While one of the detectives kept Kearney busy, the other secretly pulled a few fibers from the carpet for testing

The evidence had, of course, been obtained illegally and would therefore be inadmissible in court. But that had never been the intention. The police only wanted an indication of whether Kearney and Hill were viable suspects. Forensic tests run on the fibers would prove that they were.

The visit by the police had spooked Patrick Kearney. Immediately after the officers left, he began destroying all of the newspaper cuttings he'd collected on the Trash Bag Killer Case and discarding his collection of serial killer literature. When the police called again and asked him and Hill to supply samples of their pubic hair, he decided that it was time to run. By the time officers arrived with a search warrant for the premises, Kearney and Hill were long gone.

Police nonetheless searched the apartment, turning up a hacksaw that contained minute traces of human blood and tissue. They also found rolls of nylon filament tape and garbage bags similar to those used in the Trash Bag Murders. But the most damning evidence was found in the bathroom. Here police uncovered traces of human blood, undetectable to the naked eye, but clearly visible when exposed to Luminol.

The pressure was now on to find the fugitives and their photographs were distributed to law enforcement agencies across the country. Kearney and Hill had meanwhile fled to El Paso, Texas, but Kearney had already decided that he wasn't suited to a life on the run. At the urging of relatives, he and Hill returned to California.

On July 1, 1977, Kearney and Hill marched into the offices of the Riverside County Sheriff, where Kearney pointed to a "Wanted" poster bearing their image and declared to the astonished desk sergeant, "We're them." They were immediately placed under arrest and charged with two counts of murder, bail set at $500,000 each.

Kearney cooperated fully with the police, telling officers that he found hurting and killing people sexually exciting. "The murders excited me and gave me a feeling of dominance," he confessed.

At one point during the interrogation, officers asked him about drugging and torturing his victims. Kearney seemed, at first, confused, and then affronted. "I am not the Wooden Stake," he declared indignantly. The police had assumed that Kearney was responsible for the murders committed by sadistic "Scorecard Killer," Randy Kraft, who was still at large at the time. Kearney appeared insulted at the suggestion that he would torture his victims.

Eventually, the matter came to trial, with the grand jury refusing to indict David Hill and Riverside District Attorney, Byron Morton, saying that information unearthed by investigators seemed to exonerate Hill. Kearney, too, confirmed that Hill was neither involved in, nor aware of, the murders.

Acting against the advice of his attorney, who advised him to plead not guilty by reason of insanity, Patrick Kearney entered guilty pleas to all of the charges against him. He also asked to be sentenced immediately, apparently because he believed that it would rule out the possibility of the death penalty (a moot point, all of Kearney's crimes had been committed while the death penalty was suspended in California).

Patrick Kearney was eventually convicted on 21 counts of murder and received a life sentence for each charge. He is currently serving his time at the California State Prison in Mule Creek and will never be released.

Edmund Kemper

The Co-ed Killer

"This craving, this awful raging eating feeling inside, this fantastic passion. It was overwhelming me. It was like drugs. It was like alcohol. A little wasn't enough." - Ed Kemper

The beautiful beach community of Santa Cruz lies south of San Francisco on the Pacific Coast. It is a haven for tourists, surrounded as it is, by majestic mountains, rugged coastline, and towering redwood trees. But in the early 1970's, Santa Cruz acquired a rather less desirable reputation. It became known as "Murder City," or alternately, "The Murder Capital of the World."

And with good reason too, during this time a trio of deadly psychopaths stalked the small town. First, there was John Linley Frazier, a crazed hippy who murdered five people in a bloody spree in 1970. Then there was Herb Mullin, a deeply psychotic young man who murdered 13 people in the belief that it would prevent an earthquake. And finally, there was Edmund Emil Kemper III – 6 foot 9 inches, 300 pounds, of murderous fury, a killer and mutilator of 10, including his own mother and grandparents.

Edmund Kemper was born in Burbank, California on December 18, 1948, the middle child, and only son, of Edmund Kemper Jr. and his wife, Clarnell. Ed was close to his father and devastated when his parents divorced in 1957. Shortly thereafter, Clarnell moved the family to Montana, and it was there that Edmund's problems first began to manifest.

By the time he was ten, Ed was already developing violent fantasies about murdering his mother, fantasies which soon branched out to include all women. He began to play bizarre games where he pretended to be executed in the gas chamber. He would cut the heads off his sisters' dolls. On one occasion his sister teased him about having a crush on his teacher. She asked Ed why he didn't kiss her, to which the 10-year-old replied, "If I did that, I'd have to kill her first."

These were worrying signs in a child so young, and his mother didn't help. She constantly berated and harangued Edmund, even locking him in the cellar because she believed he might harm his sisters. When he was 13, Kemper killed and decapitated the family cat, placing its head on a stick. At around the same time he ran away from home. He wanted to live with his father, but by now Kemper Sr. was remarried, with a new family. He allowed Ed to stay for a day or two, before sending him back to his mother. Her solution was to pack Edmund off to his paternal grandparent's ranch in North Fork, California.

Edmund hated it in North Fork. He found his grandmother as argumentative and as dominant as his mother and the two quarreled frequently. Matters eventually came to a head on August 27, 1964, eight months after Kemper had moved in. On that August afternoon, the 15-year-old boy (already an awkward, gangly, six-foot-four), got into yet another argument with his grandmother, Maude. Enraged, Kemper fetched the .22 rifle he'd been given as a Christmas present and shot the 66-year-old woman in the head. Then he waited for his grandfather to return from the grocery store and shot him too. Later he'd say that he'd killed his grandmother to "see how it feels," and his grandfather to "spare him the anguish of finding his wife dead."

Not knowing what else to do, Kemper then called his mother in Montana and told her what he had done. She instructed him to call the police, which he did, waiting calmly at the ranch until they arrived.

Kemper was placed with the California Youth Authority. Then he was sent for psychiatric evaluation, diagnosed as a paranoid schizophrenic, and transferred to the Atascadero State Hospital for the Criminally Insane, where he would remain until his release on his 21st birthday. Psychiatrists strongly recommended that Kemper should not live with his mother, but given that he had no place else to go, he moved back in with Clarnell in 1969.

Kemper's mother had just divorced her third husband and taken a job as an administrative assistant at the new university in Santa Cruz. She'd recently moved into a duplex on Ord Drive in Aptos, when Ed came to stay with her. Before long, they were back into their old routine, getting into fierce arguments that the neighbors could hear through the walls. Kemper would later say that his mother was constantly on his case, bickering and sniping and criticizing everything he did, attacking his manhood and his sense of worth.

As part of his parole requirements, Kemper attended a community college and did well. He hoped to be accepted into the police force but was turned down because he was too tall. Disappointed, he began hanging out at "The Jury Room," a bar frequented by police officers. There, he became well known to many of the cops. He was polite and soft-spoken, his speech intelligent and articulate. The cops liked him, and gave him the nickname, "Big Ed."

Kemper worked at several short-term jobs during this time, before landing a position with the California Highway Department. Soon he'd saved enough money to move out of his mother's home. He relocated to Alameda, near San Francisco, sharing an apartment with a friend. He bought a motorcycle, but his childhood clumsiness hadn't left him and he was involved in two accidents, one of which earned him a $15,000 insurance payout.

With this unexpected windfall, Kemper bought a yellow Ford Galaxy and began to cruise the highways. He also started picking up female hitchhikers, learning how to sweet-talk them into his car, how to allay any fears they might have about his huge bulk. By his own estimation, he picked up as many as 150 female hikers without harming any of them. But, gradually, he began to prepare his vehicle for what he had in mind, stocking it with plastic bags, knives, a blanket, and handcuffs. The need was growing. Finally, when his drive to kill became too much, he acted.

According to Kemper's later confession, his first attempts at killing hitchhikers met with failure. He said he'd pick up a girl and drive her to a remote spot, only to realize that he couldn't go through with it. That changed on May 7, 1972. On that day, Kemper picked up two 18-year-old college students named Mary Anne Pesce and Anita Luchessa. The girls were hiking to Stanford, about an hour away, and were grateful for the ride. But that gratitude soon turned to terror as Kemper pulled off the highway and stopped on a dirt road. Using a gun to keep the women quiet, he told them he was going to rape them, then handcuffed Pesce in the back seat, and forced Luchessa into the trunk. He then placed a bag over Pesce's head and tried to strangle her, but she struggled so much that he drew his knife and began stabbing her, delivering blow after blow as the terrified woman screamed in pain and terror. Eventually, Kemper cut her throat, then went to the trunk, dragged out Anita Luchessa and killed her too.

Carrying out the murders had not gone as smoothly as he had imagined in his fantasies, but he now had what he wanted, two corpses under his control, all his. Kemper moved the bodies into the trunk and drove back to his apartment. On the way home he was pulled over by a highway patrolman for a broken taillight, but he remained calm and co-operative and got off with a warning. He said later that if the officer had asked him to open the trunk, he'd have killed him on the spot.

Kemper's roommate was out when he got to the apartment, so he wrapped the bodies in blankets and carried them upstairs. Once inside, he laid the dead girls out on the floor of his bedroom, where he photographed them. Then he began dismembering the corpses, stopping to take photographs and to perform sexual acts on them. Later, he packed the body parts into bags and buried them in a shallow grave in the mountains. His final outrage was to use Mary Anne Pesce's severed head for fellatio, before discarding it in a ravine.

After the double murder, Kemper went back to picking up female hikers and delivering them safely to their destinations. He would even warn his passengers against accepting rides from strangers. But the need was growing again. On September 14, 1972, he gave in to it.

Aiko Koo was a fifteen-year-old schoolgirl who had just missed the bus and was late for a dance class. She was grateful when Kemper picked her up but soon regretted accepting the ride as he drove right past the dance studio and kept going. Eventually, he stopped on a remote road where he produced a gun and told the terrified girl that he was going to rape her. Koo immediately started screaming and Kemper, perhaps confused by this turn of events, scrambled out of the car and slammed the door accidentally locking himself out.

Koo was now locked inside the vehicle with the keys and Kemper's gun. Had she been thinking clearly, she might have used the weapon to protect herself or perhaps even driven off and left Kemper stranded. Instead, she allowed Kemper to sweet talk her into opening the door. He responded by immediately grabbing her by the throat and strangling her to death. Thereafter, he raped her corpse before stuffing it in the trunk and driving off. On the way home, he even made a stop at his favorite bar to talk with his cop buddies. Then he drove to his apartment where he photographed and decapitated Koo and had sex with her headless corpse.

The day after he killed Aiko Koo, Ed Kemper went before a panel of psychiatrists, as required by the conditions of his parole. The panel noted that he'd done well in school, that he had a steady job, and that he'd stayed out of trouble. Kemper, by now well versed in the whole psychiatric evaluation routine, told them exactly what they wanted to hear. Suitably impressed, they declared Ed "normal," "safe," and, "no danger to anyone." Yet even as the psychiatrists signed the order sealing his juvenile record, Kemper was keeping a deadly secret. In the trunk of his car, parked downstairs in the lot, lay the severed head of Aiko Koo.

Having been given a clean bill of mental health, Kemper drove away and buried Koo's remains near Boulder Creek. Then he lay low for a while, fueling his fantasies with the sickening photographs he'd taken of his three victims. But the pressure soon began to build, and before long he began hunting for another victim.

On January 7, 1973, Kemper offered a ride to a pretty, 19-year-old student, named Cindy Schall. He drove her to a secluded spot where he produced a .22 pistol and shot her in the head. By now, Kemper was again living with his mother, so he drove back to her house, where he dismembered Schall's body in the bathtub. He kept the remains in his room overnight, before burying the head in the backyard and later throwing the body parts over a cliff. They quickly washed up on a beach, but no one suspected Kemper. He was free to kill again.

On February 5, after yet another argument with his mother, Kemper picked up Rosalind Thorpe. Then, with Thorpe in the passenger seat, he picked up another student, Allison Liu. Following his now established M.O., Kemper waited until they were in a remote area, then pulled over, ostensibly to admire the view. As Thorpe turned to look, Kemper removed a pistol from the side panel and shot her in the head, killing her instantly. He then turned and fired four shots at Liu, sitting in the back seat, hitting her in the hand and in the temple.

Like most serial killers, Kemper had refined his methodology with each successive kill. He quickly dragged the bodies to the trunk and mopped up any blood in the car. Then he drove back to his mother's house, where he spent the night in an orgy of necrophilia and dismemberment, capturing every sickening act on camera. The following morning, he scattered the remains, dropping some in the ocean, others in the woods and tossing the heads away separately.

Kemper had now killed and dismembered six young women in the space of just over a year. Although the police at this stage had no leads in the case and did not regard him as a suspect, he sensed that they were closing in. An officer he knew, Sergeant Aluffi, had called at his house just days before, to question him about a weapon he owned, and Kemper also feared that his mother might have found some of the souvenirs he'd taken from his victims.

On April 20, 1973, Clarnell went out with friends for the evening and came home slightly tipsy. Kemper, by now increasingly paranoid, was lying awake when she got in. He had decided to murder his mother, to save her from the embarrassment of learning that he was the "Coed Killer."

After Clarnell retired to bed, he crept into her room holding a claw hammer which he used to bludgeon her to death. He then decapitated the corpse and placed the head on a mantel where he threw darts at it. He also cut out his mother's vocal cords and dropped them in the garbage disposal. But the machine couldn't break down the tough vocal tissue and ejected it back up into the sink. "That seemed appropriate," Kemper later said, "as much as she'd bitched and screamed and yelled at me over so many years."

Kemper knew now that the game was up and that he'd be arrested for his mother's murder. But his lust for killing was still not sated. He therefore placed a call to his mother's best friend, asking her to come over to the house urgently. The minute 59-year-old Sally Hallett entered, Kemper overpowered her and strangled her to death. Then he stripped her naked and beheaded her. He spent that night in the house performing depravities on the two corpses. The following morning, he fled in Sally Hallet's car.

Kemper drove east, leaving California and passing through Nevada and Utah, all the while tuned in to the radio, hoping to hear news that the bodies had been discovered. When no news came, he decided to initiate the discovery himself. Stopping at a phone booth in Pueblo, Colorado, he called the Santa Cruz Police Department and confessed to the murders of his mother and Sally Hallet. At first, police thought it was a crank call, but Kemper phoned back and asked to speak to a detective he knew. Then he waited patiently at the phone booth for officers to arrive and arrest him, one of the few instances where a serial killer has willingly surrendered himself to the authorities.

Once in custody, Kemper quickly confessed to the "Coed Killings," and led investigators to the remains of his victims. He went on trial in October 1973, charged with eight murders. On November 8, the jury deliberated for five hours before finding Kemper guilty on all counts. He asked for the death penalty but with the moratorium in place on capital punishment at the time, he was sentenced to life imprisonment without the possibility of parole.

Edmund Kemper is currently serving his term at California Medical Facility in Vacaville. He has stated on several occasions that he never wants to be released for fear that he will kill again.

Bobby Joe Long

The Classified Ads Rapist

"Yes, I killed them. I did them all." – Bobby Joe Long

Bobby Joe Long was born on October 15, 1953 in Kenova, West Virginia. His mother, Louella, was just 17 years old at the time of his birth and within two years she had divorced Bobby Joe's father. She then moved to Miami, taking her son with her. But life in Florida was hard. Louella earned a pittance at her various waitressing jobs and the family lived in poverty. In fact, they were so poor that they could only afford one bed. Bobby ended up sharing that bed with his mother well into his teens. The only exception was when Louella brought a man home. Then the boy was relegated to the couch and had to listen to his mother and her one-night stand loudly making love. Many of these men were also cruel to the youngster, leaving him with a smoldering anger.

That, however, was not the worst of Bobby Joe's problems. At age seven, he ran out into the road and was struck by a car, leaving him with a deformed jaw. That made him a target for schoolyard bullies. He also had medical problems, an extra X chromosome that produced abnormal amounts of estrogen and caused him to grow breasts. These had to be surgically removed. Meanwhile, his father had reappeared on the scene and his parents' on-again-off-again relationship only added to tensions in the home. Brief periods of stability with both parents were punctuated by his mother's steady stream of short term lovers. Bobby, by now old enough to understand, begged her to dress and behave more conservatively. Louella laughed him off.

It has been noted that in the development of many serial killers there is a strained relationship with a dominant mother. It has also been observed that the fledgling killer acts out in predictable ways. He begins setting fires and hurting animals; he starts fantasizing about hurting women, who serve as surrogates for the overbearing mother. Bobby Joe Long did all of these things.

The final piece of the jigsaw that turned Bobby Joe Long into a serial killer occurred in 1974 when he was 21 years old. By now married to a childhood sweetheart, Long was riding his motorcycle when he was involved in a collision with a car that left him with a fractured skull and other serious injuries. He would spend the next six months recuperating in hospital, eventually making a full recovery. However, the head injury had left him with a strange affliction, a compulsive and overriding sex drive. Such were his demands that his wife, Cynthia, found it impossible to satisfy him. Frustrated Long turned his attentions elsewhere. In late 1974, he was accused of rape, although the charge was later reduced to assault and the sentence involved probation rather than jail time.

After completing his period of judicial supervision, Long moved his family to Tampa where over the next two years, Cynthia gave birth to two children. Long, meanwhile, was attending college, working towards a radiologist qualification. It all looked rosy on the outside but behind the scenes, the marriage was deeply troubled. Cynthia had begun to resist Long's constant demands for sex. He, in response, had begun beating her and committing spousal rape. Then, while reading the classified ads in the Tampa Tribune one day, Bobby Joe hit upon a new way of servicing his insatiable sex drive. He realized that responding to any of the advertisements would give him easy and unfettered access to a stranger's home. Shortly after, the Florida newspapers started running stories about a terrifying intruder known as the 'Classified Ad Rapist.'

In November 1979, Bobby Joe Long graduated with an associate degree in X-ray technology. Such qualifications are highly sought after. In a short time, he'd been recruited by a Miami Beach hospital. There, he quickly developed a reputation for sexual harassment towards female employees, resulting in a warning from his supervisor. Rather than stop, however, Long shifted his focus. He began fondling patients, a habit that led eventually to his dismissal. Cynthia, also, had had enough by now. She filed for divorce.

It was the rejection Bobby Joe had experienced at the hands of his mother all over again and he responded in much the same way. In the months that followed, there was an escalation in Classified Ad Rapist attacks. Long also took some outrageous risks, for example, raping a woman from whom he was renting a room. The woman went straight to the police and Long was arrested, although his conviction was later overturned on appeal. In January 1982, he moved back to West Virginia to live with his parents. Deeply unhappy, he contemplated suicide until a surprise job offer lifted his spirits.

The job was in his chosen field and was at a hospital in Huntington, Virginia. Bobby Joe started work determined to keep his urges under control and to make a go of this new opportunity. And for a while, he succeeded. His employers were impressed by what they saw and he even started dating one of his co-workers. But all too soon, old impulses got the better of him and a familiar pattern ensued. First nurses started reporting inappropriate behavior. Then female patients began complaining of being instructed to strip, even when the X-ray did not require it. Forced into action, hospital administrators convened a disciplinary board and Long was dismissed. He departed that same day for Florida.

The Tampa area had enjoyed a respite from the 'Classified Ad Rapist' for over a year but with Bobby Joe Long back in town the attacks resumed with a vengeance. Detectives investigating the case also picked up a familiar pattern. The attacks always occurred on weekdays, when women were more likely to be home alone. There was another reason for the weekday attacks. Bobby Joe had secured another medical job, working weekends at a Tampa Bay clinic.

Bizarrely, while carrying out his reign of terror, Long had become a born-again Christian, courtesy of a nurse he was dating. And that reign of terror was about to see an escalation. Bobby Joe Long was about to make the leap from serial rapist to serial killer.

On May 13, 1984, a couple of boys were crossing a field close to the I-75, near Tampa, when they came across the corpse of a woman. Capt. Gary Terry and Detective Lee Baker of the

Hillsborough County Sheriff's Office were called to the scene and discovered a badly decomposed body.

The corpse was bound, had a noose around the neck, and had been explicitly posed. An autopsy would reveal that the woman had been raped and severely beaten prior to her death. There were significant forensic clues left at the scene – an unusual tire track, and a number of red fibers.

Capt. Terry felt that the fibers might be an important piece of evidence and contacted Special Agent Michael P. Malone, an expert on fiber analysis at the FBI. Malone agreed to examine the fibers and concluded that they were from a cheap type of carpeting used in automobiles.

The police had meanwhile fingerprinted the corpse and identified her as 20-year-old, Ngeun Thi Long (a.k.a. Lana Long), a dancer at the Sly Fox Lounge in Tampa. She had last been seen leaving a bar called CCs.

Investigators initially suspected Lana Long's boyfriend, who had been known to beat her. However, he had an ironclad alibi for the time of death and police were left to conclude that this was just a random murder – a tragic case of the victim being in the wrong place at the wrong time.

That theory held for less than two weeks. Then, a second body turned up.

On May 27, 1984, a construction worker discovered a nude female corpse near Plant City in Hillsborough County. Detectives arriving at the scene were immediately struck by similarities to the Lana Long case.

The woman was nude, with her hands bound behind her back and a noose around her neck. She'd been stabbed, strangled, and beaten to death. As with the other crime scene, there were significant trace elements – red carpet fibers, several strands of hair, and tire tracks similar to those found at the previous murder site.

The autopsy would reveal the full brutality of the crime. The victim's skull had received five massive blows and a major artery in the neck had been severed. Either of those injuries would probably have been fatal, but the killer had also strangled the victim. The official cause of death was given as strangulation and severe head trauma.

The victim was identified as Michelle Denise Simms, a 22-year-old prostitute and drug addict. Given the similarities between the M.O. in this and the Lana Long case, police began to fear that they might have a serial killer on their hands. When the carpet fibers were forensically matched to those found at the first scene, that suspicion was confirmed.

The next step in the investigation was to contact the FBI's Behavioral Science Unit for a profile of the killer. BSU believed the murderer to be a Caucasian male, mid-20s, sociable, outgoing, and manipulative. He would be self-centered and impulsive with a macho persona. His education would be high school at best and he'd have a spotty work record with multiple short-term employments. He'd probably have a woman in his life, but he'd be unfaithful and would brag about his sexual exploits.

It was likely that he'd have a criminal record. If he'd done jail time, he would have been a model prisoner. He was an organized killer, meaning he relied on manipulation and sweet talk to get women into his car. Once he had them in his clutches, he'd keep them alive for some time. He was a sadist, who enjoyed torturing his victims physically and psychologically. If he wasn't caught soon, he would definitely kill again.

This profile would later prove to be mostly accurate, although Long, of course, had more than a high school diploma, he was a certified X-ray technician. Between his second and third murders, he'd also secured a new job in the medical field, this time at Tampa General Hospital. There he performed mainly mammograms, which was right up Long's alley. Staring at naked breasts all day filled him with lustful urges. After his shift was over he'd go cruising, looking for release.

Elizabeth Loudenback, 22, had disappeared from the mobile park where she lived, on June 8, 1984. Her mother had reported her missing almost immediately, but it would be more than two weeks before her severely decomposed body was found.

An autopsy revealed that she'd been strangled, but unlike the earlier two victims, she was fully clothed, and no ropes were found at the scene. Elizabeth was not a prostitute or a dancer, and the dumpsite was different, a fair distance from the Interstate. In fact, investigators might not have linked this murder to the series at all, had it not been for the distinctive red fibers found on Elizabeth's clothing.

On September 27, 1974, Long was fired from his job at Tampa General. The reason was a familiar one, complaints from nursing staff and female patients about his wandering hands and sexually suggestive comments. Three days after his dismissal, he killed again.

On October 7, four months after the murder of Elizabeth Loudenback, a ranch hand found the decomposed corpse of a woman on a farm north of Hillsborough State Park. The victim was identified via her fingerprints as Chanel Devon Williams, an 18-year-old prostitute. She'd been raped and strangled, then killed with a gunshot to the back of the head. Trace evidence at the scene included semen stains, a Caucasian pubic hair, and the now familiar, red carpet fibers.

A week later, on October 14, a fifth body was discovered in northeastern Hillsborough County. Fingerprints identified her as Karen Beth Dinsfriend, 28, a known prostitute. She'd been strangled and the killer had left behind his familiar forensic calling card, including the red fibers found at the other murder sites.

And still, the bodies kept turning up. On October 28, Kimberly Kyle Hoops, a 22-year-old prostitute, who went by the street name Sugar, was found. Then on November 6, 1984, the corpse of 18-year-old Virginia Lee Johnson was discovered. Johnson had been a prostitute on the Tampa Strip. Six days later, a sign painter in Tampa came across the body of Kim Marie Swann, 21. Like the first victim, Lana Long, she had been a dancer at the Sly Fox Lounge on the Tampa Strip.

The police worked the case hard, placing high-risk areas under surveillance, warning sex workers to be vigilant, revisiting the evidence and the BSU profile again and again. But the killer remained elusive. Investigators badly needed a break. On November 3, they got one.

On the evening of that day, 17-year-old Lisa McVey was riding her bicycle along a quiet street when a car pulled in front of her, cutting her off. A man got out holding a gun and ordered her to get into his vehicle, where he bound and blindfolded her. As the terrified girl begged the abductor not to kill her, he stripped off her clothing and then forced her to perform oral sex on him.

Afterward, the man drove around for a while, eventually bringing Lisa to his apartment. Over the next 26 hours, she was repeatedly raped, forced to perform various sex acts and even instructed to take a shower with her attacker. She was certain she was going to be killed but determined anyway to take in as many details as she could. She wanted to be able to identify her abductor should she somehow manage to escape.

Peering under her blindfold, Lisa took in details of his car, his apartment, and the location of an automatic teller machine where he stopped to get cash. She even managed to drop a hair clip next to his bed, so that she'd be able to prove later that she had been there.

Lisa also worked at gaining her attacker's trust and did her best not to get him angry, complying with all of his demands. Eventually, she sensed that he was relaxing. He was less aggressive towards her. He started calling her "Babe."

Then, after two days of captivity, he seemed to lose interest in his captive. He told her that they were leaving and walked her back to the car. Lisa felt certain that she was being driven to her death, but after a while, the abductor stopped the vehicle and told her to get out. His last words to her were, "Take care."

Lisa immediately called her father, who contacted the police. Under questioning, Lisa was able to provide them with a wealth of information.

Her attacker was white, mid-30s, with brown hair, thin eyebrows, and a mustache. He was muscular but slightly overweight and had certain mannerisms she described as, "somewhat feminine." He drove a dark red or maroon Dodge Magnum with a red steering wheel and dashboard. The seats and interior were white. She also provided details about his apartment and the bank where he'd stopped.

As the kidnapper had released Lisa alive, the police had not yet linked the abduction to the serial killer case they were working. That link was to come when the FBI lab tested the red fibers found on Lisa McVey's clothing. They were a match to those found on the serial killer victims. Thanks to McVey's presence of mind, the police now had a description of the killer and his car.

On November 15, two police officers were on patrol in Tampa when they spotted a red Dodge, matching the description of the car they were looking for. They pulled the vehicle over under the pretense of investigating a hit-and-run. The driver gave his name as Robert Joe Long and was co-operative, even allowing himself to be photographed by the officers. He seemed relieved when they let him go.

Now that they had a name to go on, investigators checked bank records and saw that Long had withdrawn cash at the time McVey said her abductor had made a withdrawal. They then checked Long's criminal record and found that he was currently on probation for aggravated assault.

Long was placed under surveillance while the police obtained the necessary warrants and put together a takedown team. He was arrested as he left a movie theater. He surrendered without a fight.

With a suspect now in custody, the painstaking task of linking him to each of the murder victims began. Forensics teams got to work on Long's vehicle and residence. The car produced a wealth of evidence, including a match to the red carpet fibers, hair and rope fibers, fingerprints, and traces of blood. Long's apartment yielded items of women's clothing, Lisa McVey's hair clip, and photos Long had taken of himself raping his victims.

Interrogated by Detectives Latimer and Price, Long admitted to kidnapping and raping Lisa McVey. However, even when confronted with the overwhelming physical evidence, he steadfastly denied involvement in the serial murders. He insisted on having an attorney present and, by law, the detectives should have ended the interview right there.

But Latimer felt that he was close to a breakthrough and decided to have one last crack at Long. He urged Long to come clean and again pointed to the strong forensic evidence against him. At this point, Long smiled at the detectives. "Well, I guess you got me good," he said. "Yes, I killed them. All the ones in the paper. I did them all."

Over the hours that followed, Bobby Joe Long went on to describe his crimes in graphic and sickening detail. He also provided information about a ninth victim, Vicky Elliot, whose body hadn't yet been discovered. And there was an unexpected bonus for detectives. For years, they'd been hunting the elusive "Classified Ads Rapist." Now Long admitted to being that man.

Describing his M.O., Long said that he would scan the classifieds to find items for sale. Then he'd make a call and arrange to view the item. If a lone woman answered the door he'd talk his way in, then bind and rape her, sometimes robbing the house on his way out. If a man was present, he'd simply view the item and then say he wasn't interested. Using this method, Long had raped between 50 and 150 women and girls, some as young as 12.

Long's confession, once transcribed, ran to 45 pages although it omitted one important point – a motive.

And yet, if anyone was destined to become a serial killer, it was Bobby Joe Long. A distant cousin of another notorious serial murderer, Henry Lee Lucas, Long's childhood and early adulthood were punctuated by traumatic episodes – severe head injuries, a confused sexual identity, an absent father, and an ambiguous relationship with his dominant mother. Add to that his abnormally high sex drive and it is not difficult to understand how he became a psychopathic sex killer.

Bobby Joe Long was charged with nine counts of murder, nine counts of sexual battery, and nine counts of kidnapping. Found guilty on all charges, he was sentenced to death, plus 34 life terms, and an additional 693 years in prison. He currently awaits execution on Florida's death row.

Earle Nelson

The Dark Strangler

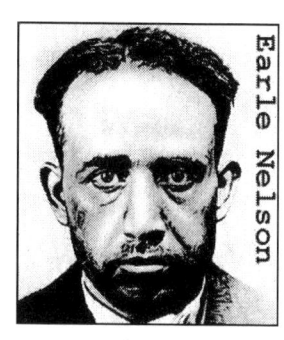

The term "serial killer" was first popularized in 1974, when famed FBI profiler, Robert Ressler, used it in a lecture to the British police academy at Bramshill, England. Earlier, author John Brophy had coined the term 'serial murderer' in his 1966 book, The Meaning of Murder, the first published usage of the term in the English language. Going even further back, Berlin police director, Ernst Gennat, used the phrase serienmörder ("serial murderer") to describe German psychopath Peter Kürten in a 1930 article.

But whatever the origin of the term, it is clear that these monsters are far from a recent phenomenon. One of the most infamous serial killer cases, in fact, dates back to the 1920's and the killing spree perpetrated by Earle Nelson, dubbed by the press the "Gorilla Killer" or the "Dark Strangler."

Earle Leonard Nelson was born with a number of strikes against his name. He never knew his mother for one thing - she died of syphilis (a disease she'd contracted from his father) in 1898, when Earle was just nine months old. And he didn't get to know his father either – he died just six months later, of the same disease.

Earle was raised in San Francisco by his widowed grandmother, a staunch Pentecostal with two young children of her own. She genuinely cared for her grandson, but he was a difficult child, hyperactive at times, and at others, depressed, obstinate, and prone to strange behavior. He seldom bothered with the conventions of personal hygiene or good manners, for example. One of his particularly unsettling habits was to drench his food in olive oil, then put his face in the plate and slurp it up. Another peculiar practice was to leave for school wearing a clean set of clothes and return wearing an entirely different – usually filthy – set. No one ever found out where he came upon these items of clothing.

Earle had other peculiarities, too. From a young age, he became obsessed with the Bible, even if he seemed to have difficulty abiding by its teachings. He was a loner, a persistent shoplifter, a daydreamer. At the age of just seven, he was expelled from school because of his fierce temper and a propensity for violence when annoyed.

At the age of 11, Earle suffered what would be the first in a series of bad head injuries. On this occasion, he was struck by a streetcar while riding a bicycle. He was knocked unconscious and remained so, between brief periods of awareness, for the next week. And there was an even more traumatic event three years later - his grandmother died, leaving him devastated. Shortly thereafter, the 14-year-old Earle was shipped off to live with his Aunt Lillian.

Not long after settling in his new home, Earle Nelson dropped out of school for the final time. He began working menial jobs, but they seldom lasted due to his eccentric behavior and inherent laziness. He seldom finished any task he was given. Often, he just wandered away from a work site and never went back.

At the age of just 15, he began regularly visiting prostitutes, spending the bulk of his meager earnings on them. The rest of his money went on booze and lurid magazines. He also started wandering, disappearing for days on end, returning home battered and bruised from brawling. Even more worryingly, he'd taken to creating imaginary acquaintances, carrying on lengthy conversations and arguments with them.

In 1915, Earle got into trouble with the law for the first time. During one of his forays around the country, he tried to break into a cabin but was surprised when the owner returned home. He fled into the woods but was soon captured. Put on trial for burglary, the 18-year-old Earle was sent down for a stint at San Quentin.

He emerged two years later and enlisted in the army under his father's surname, "Ferral". Military discipline didn't appeal to Earle, though. Within a few weeks, he was AWOL. He fled to Utah, staying there for a time before returning to California to re-enlist, this time in the U.S. Navy. A month later he was AWOL again.

Nelson signed up for a third stint in the military in 1918. However, his outlandish behavior soon drew the attention of his superiors and he was committed to Napa State Mental Hospital.

At this stage he was just 18, but already he was an alcoholic and infected with syphilis and gonorrhea. During his intake interview, he admitted that he masturbated several times a day, and had done so since the age of 13. He was also obsessed with God and religion, constantly reading the Bible and spouting verse.

Nelson would spend thirteen months at Napa, escaping twice during that time. After the third escape, the military police didn't bother looking for him. He was discharged from the Navy, with his condition noted as "improved."

His military career now over, Nelson returned to the home of his longsuffering Aunt Lillian, who took him in and found him a job as a janitor at St. Mary's Hospital, near San Francisco. A co-worker in the housekeeping department was 58-year-old Mary Martin, a spinster who resembled Earle's grandmother. The 21-year-old Earle was instantly smitten and soon asked Mary to be his wife.

Mary said yes, but before long she'd have cause to regret her decision as she became aware of her new husband's eccentricities. He refused to bathe, displayed appalling table manners, and had an insatiable sex drive. If Mary was unwilling to satisfy his needs, he'd openly masturbate in front of her (a sin according to her strict Catholic upbringing). Earle had the peculiar habit of leaving the home in one set of clothes and returning wearing something different. He was also extremely possessive, reacting furiously if Mary so much as talked to another man, even her own brother. He never struck his wife, instead taking out his fury on inanimate objects.

The next significant event in Nelson's descent towards serial murder was a second serious head injury, suffered when he fell from a ladder at work. He was hospitalized but left, against medical advice, after two days. After that, he spoke of hearing voices and seeing visions. He also became even more paranoid towards his wife, and increasingly violent. When he announced suddenly that he was leaving Palo Alto, Mary declined to go with him and stood her ground even when he begged. It was probably a wise decision.

Angered by Mary's rejection, Nelson attempted his first murder on May 19, 1921. He'd spotted 12-year-old Mary Summers playing outside her house before going in. Nelson knocked on the door claiming to be a plumber sent to fix a gas leak. Mary's older brother Charles Jr. admitted him and he went immediately to the basement, where he encountered the girl. He tried to strangle her, but she fought back and her screams alerted her brother. Nelson then fled the scene, but was soon arrested. Once in custody, his behavior so stunned his jailers that they arranged for him to be transferred to the city hospital in a straitjacket.

A month later, Nelson appeared before a judge to determine his competency to stand trial. Psychiatrists who examined him described him variously as "apathetic, eccentric, noisy, destructive, incendiary, restless, violent, dangerous, excited and depressed." They said he was dangerous to himself and others and declared that he should not be at large. The judge had no option but to commit him to the Napa State Hospital — a place he'd broken out of three times in the past.

Nelson's second stretch at Napa would last four years, during which time he escaped only once and was quickly recaptured. When he was eventually released he persuaded his wife to take him back. But he stayed only a few weeks before he hit the road. Earle Nelson was about to make the transition from petty criminal to serial murderer.

The first woman to fall victim to the "Dark Strangler" was Clara Newmann, a 62-year-old widow, who ran a boarding house in San Francisco. Nelson, wandering the streets, saw a "To Rent" sign in her front window and knocked on the door to enquire about it. He was polite and courteous and Mrs. Newmann had no problem admitting him to view the room.

A while later, the landlady's nephew, Merton Newmann Sr., went down to the basement to check on the furnace. He was passed in the passage by a large man heading towards the door. Merton asked if he could help, to which the man responded, "Tell the landlady I will return in an hour. I wish to rent the bedroom."

Merton thought nothing of it and returned to his room. Several hours later he went downstairs to speak to his aunt. She was nowhere to be found and none of the residents reported having seen her. Alarmed now, Merton began a search of the house, assisted by some of the boarders. They soon found Clara Newmann in a vacant attic apartment, her clothes bunched up around her waist. An autopsy would reveal that she'd been strangled by bare hands and had been raped after death.

A little over two weeks later, another landlady was murdered, this time in nearby San Jose. The circumstances of Laura Beal's death were almost identical to those of Clara Newmann and the papers immediately began reporting that it was the work of the same man. This sparked a deluge of tips from the public, none of which got the police any closer to identifying the killer.

A month passed without significant progress but also without any further murders. The public began to relax. Then, on June 16,

1926, the killer struck again, strangling and violating Mrs. Lillian St. Mary at the boarding house she ran.

By now, the police knew that they were looking for the same perpetrator in all three murders, but still they had nothing much to go on – a large, dark-complexioned man was described at or near the various crime scenes, but that was no help in identifying the killer. The press picked up on the description, though, and began dubbing him "The Dark Strangler." A police warning went out to landladies, cautioning them against showing a room to any man alone. At the same time, the police chief confidently announced that they'd make an arrest soon. Unbeknownst to him, his quarry had already slipped the net.

With the city of San Francisco gripped by panic, Nelson made his way south to Santa Barbara. There, he enquired about a room at a boarding house run by Mrs. Ollie Russell. A while later, Mrs. Russell's husband, alerted by a complaint from a resident about a banging noise, discovered his wife's body. She'd been strangled with a loop of chord that was so tightly wound that it had cut into her throat. She'd also been sexually assaulted.

And still the killings continued, in August, 50-year-old Oakland resident, Mary Nisbet, was throttled to death. Then 30-year-old Beata Whithers of Portland, Oregon was killed. Just two days later, Virginia Grant was murdered, raped and robbed in her home. A few days after, Mabel Fluke was found strangled and sexually assaulted, her body concealed in an attic crawl space.

Over the next 16 months, Earle Nelson remained at large, crisscrossing the American Northwest as the body count mounted. He visited San Francisco, Oakland, Stockton, and Portland, leaving police baffled as to who the Dark Strangler was, and where he would strike next.

Even with constant warnings in the media, some women foolishly allowed him into their homes, taken in by his good manners and apparent courteousness. By the end of 1926, Nelson had killed 14 women and an eight-month-old baby.

And yet, sometimes, Nelson left potential victims alive. In one instance, he stayed at a Portland boarding house and impressed the two elderly proprietors with his good manners and knowledge of the Bible. He offered a diamond ring in payment for his board, which turned out to have been stolen from Mary Nisbet.

With the Northwest in a state of virtual siege, Nelson headed east, stopping in Iowa, Kansas City, and Philadelphia, where he killed a 60-year-old woman. He then made his way to Buffalo, New York, Detroit and Chicago before turning west again. He'd already killed 20 women in the United States - now he was heading for Canada.

Nelson crossed the border and made his way to Winnipeg, where he found lodgings with Mrs. Catherine Hill on Smith Street. But immediately, he started making mistakes that would lead to his eventual downfall. For one thing, Winnipeg was a small town, where strangers stood out. Nelson, with his hulking frame, dark complexion, and accent, was easy to spot. Neither did he try, particularly, to keep a low profile. He had a substantial bankroll (stolen from one of his victims) and he wasn't afraid to flash it around. He was also known to engage strangers in conversation on the streetcars.

This kind of behavior is typical of serial killers. They begin to believe that they are invincible and that they'll never be caught. As a result, they disregard the caution with which they committed their early crimes. No doubt, Nelson felt this way because his next murder was outside his usual M.O.

Lola Cowan was a 14-year-old schoolgirl who went door-to-door selling paper flowers to supplement her family's meager income. No one is sure exactly how she encountered Nelson, but she disappeared while calling on houses in the street where he was boarding.

Soon after, the killer claimed another victim, forcing his way into the home of Emily Patterson, strangling and then raping her. William Patterson arrived home to find his wife missing and after conducting a search of the house found her body concealed under their marital bed.

The police were alerted and they immediately conducted a sweep of all boarding houses in the city, certain that the infamous Dark Strangler had made his way to Canada. In Nelson's room on Smith Street, they discovered the decomposing body of Lola Cowan hidden under the bed.

But Nelson, now going by the name "Woodcoats," had already fled town and was heading back towards the border. A reward of $1,500 was offered for information and it paid dividends when a storeowner in Wakopa recognized him and alerted the authorities. When the local constable arrived with his revolver drawn, Nelson immediately surrendered.

Within weeks of his capture, Earle Nelson was charged with murders in San Francisco, Portland, Detroit, Philadelphia, and Buffalo. It was clear, however, that he'd never see the inside of an American courtroom. The Canadian authorities were determined to prosecute and punish him for the murders he had committed there.

There was still time for one final twist, though. Nelson had always been adept at escaping from custody, and he managed to pick the lock in his jail cell and go on the run for a few days before he was recaptured.

Earle Nelson went on trial for the murders of Lola Cowan and Emily Patterson in November 1927, and despite his proclamations of innocence, there was never any doubt as to the outcome. He went to the gallows on January 13, 1928, maintaining to the end that he was innocent.

Joel Rifkin

The New York Ripper

"I had sex with her, then things went bad and I strangled her. Do you think I need a lawyer?" – Joel Rifkin

Fictional serial killers are usually portrayed as powerful, almost mythical beings, with hyper-intelligence and superhuman strength. Joel Rifkin was anything but – a nerdy, bespectacled loser who in his mid-thirties was still living at home with his mother. And yet, he is one of the most prolific murderers in the history of New York State. And he would undoubtedly have continued killing, but for a chance traffic stop.

At 3:15 a.m. on June 28, 1993, New York state troopers Sean Ruane and Deborah Spaargaren were patrolling Long Island's Southern State Parkway when they spotted a pickup with no rear license plate. The troopers flashed the driver to stop, then used the loudspeaker, ordering him to pull over.

But the driver didn't stop. Instead, he accelerated down the next off ramp. The officers followed, called for backup and stayed on his tail during a wild 20-minute chase that ended when the pickup slammed into a telephone pole. The driver offered no resistance as police asked him to step from the truck and frisked him.

He was Joel David Rifkin, according to his driver's license, a 34-year-old resident of East Meadow, Long Island. When asked why he'd tried to flee, he made no reply, but officers were soon to find out the answer to that question. They detected a foul smell coming from the bed of the truck. Drawing back the tarp that covered it, they found the naked, decomposing corpse of a woman.

Rifkin was taken into custody and booked at Hempstead, where homicide detectives began questioning him. Asked about the dead woman, Rifkin said she was a prostitute he'd picked up and had sex with. "Then things went bad and I killed her," he said. "Do you think I need a lawyer?" He then went on to describe the murder in clinical detail, ending with a surprise for the investigating officers. He told them that this was his 17th victim.

At 8 p.m. that morning, officers arrived at the house Rifkin shared with his mother and presented Jeanne Rifkin with a search warrant. When they left six hours later, they'd discovered over 200 pieces of evidence, including jewelry, photographs, women's clothing, makeup cases, wallets, and pocketbooks, plus various ID documents including the driver's licenses of a number of female victims of unsolved homicides.

In Rifkin's garage, they found three ounces of human blood pooled in a wheelbarrow, a stockpile of rope and tarp, and a chainsaw speckled with bits of blood and human flesh. Detectives had just captured the worst serial killer in New York's history.

Joel Rifkin was born on January 20, 1959. His parents were unmarried college students who were unprepared for parenthood. They put the baby up for adoption and he was taken in by Bernard and Jeanne Rifkin, a couple from upstate New York. The Rifkins also later adopted a daughter.

In 1962, the family moved to East Meadow, Long Island, where a couple of years later, Joel entered Prospect Avenue Elementary School. The bespectacled, introverted Joel was an instant target for bullies. His classmates called him 'The Turtle' because of his slouched posture and slow movements. He became the butt of every cruel prank, excluded from games, constantly harassed, his lunch and books stolen, his pants pulled down. He also did poorly at his studies despite a tested IQ of 128. (He'd later be diagnosed with dyslexia.)

And things got even worse when Joel moved up to East Meadow High School. The jokes and pranks got crueler and more frequent. He had his head shoved into countless toilet bowls, his clothes were stolen while he was in gym class. On one occasion he took a girl to a pizza parlor and the local bullies chased him and his date from the restaurant, on another, they pelted him with eggs and locked him in the gym.

Rifkin tried to fit in. He signed up for the track team, only to be saddled with the nickname, Lard Ass. Then he joined the yearbook staff, putting in most of the work to get the publication out, only to be excluded from the year-end wrap party. Joel was deeply hurt by this latest rejection and his parents compensated by buying him a car for his birthday.

With his new wheels, Rifkin was soon trolling for hookers in nearby Hempstead. But already, his ideas about sex had been severely warped. He began developing rape and bondage fantasies. After watching Alfred Hitchcock's Frenzy, about a serial killer who terrorizes London, Rifkin began fantasizing about strangling prostitutes.

Rifkin graduated high school in 1977, finishing near the bottom of his class. Over the next six years, he attended various institutions of higher learning, each time dropping out before gaining a qualification. And his work record was no better. He was fired from any number of jobs for his absenteeism, incompetence, and poor personal hygiene. He moved out of his parents' home several times only to return when he lost yet another job and found himself unable to cope financially. He had dreams of being a writer but never advanced beyond a few stanzas of bleak poetry.

All of his spare time was spent cruising the streets. He now ranged further afield, heading into Manhattan to spend whatever money he had on prostitutes. But even here, he was a failure. He was robbed on many occasions by hookers and their pimps, and was once arrested for soliciting an undercover policewoman.

Another formative event occurred in 1987, when Rifkin's father died after a long battle with bowel cancer. Joel was devastated, lapsing into deep depression. He delivered a moving, self-penned eulogy at the funeral.

In 1988, Rifkin enrolled in a horticulture program at the State College of Technology in Farmingdale, New York. For the first time in his life, he excelled academically, making straight A's and earning an internship at the prestigious Planting Fields Arboretum in Oyster Bay, New York. Here, Joel met a fellow student who he was strongly attracted to. But he lacked the nerve to ask her out, fearing another rejection in a life littered with them. He spent his time instead, concocting a fantasy in which she declared her love for him. When this didn't materialize he became increasingly frustrated until it was just too much to bear. Joel Rifkin craved a release. He would get it by committing murder.

In March 1989, while his mother was out of town, Rifkin picked up a hooker in Manhattan and took her back to Long Island. After they had sex, the woman (who he remembers only as Susie) demanded that he take her to buy drugs. Angered by this demand, Rifkin picked up an ornamental howitzer shell and began battering her with it. Susie fought back, biting one of his fingers to the bone before he managed to subdue her. He then strangled her to death.

Like most serial killers committing their first murder, Rifkin was elated by the kill but panicked about what to do next. After wrapping the corpse in plastic trash bags, he promptly fell asleep, exhausted by his efforts. When he woke, several hours later, he dragged the body to the laundry where he began dismembering it with an X-Acto knife. He even severed her fingertips and pulled out her teeth with pliers to prevent identification. He then jammed the severed head into a paint tin and packed the remaining body parts in garbage bags. These were dumped at various locations.

Over the weeks that followed, Rifkin existed in a state of nervous anxiety. He half expected the police to come knocking at his door, but they didn't. He'd gotten away with murder.

Rifkin waited more than a year before he claimed his next victim, a prostitute by the name of Julie Blackbird. He killed her at his home again, battering her to death with a table leg. After she was dead, he considered having sex with her corpse, in emulation of Ted Bundy, but he couldn't bring himself to do it. Instead, he dismembered her, weighted the pieces down with concrete and dropped them in the East River. The body would never be found.

In April 1991, Rifkin started his own landscaping business and rented space at a local nursery to store his equipment. He approached the enterprise with his usual lackluster effort, and the business would be short lived. But the rented space would come in handy as a place for storing corpses in transit. And Rifkin would need it. The pace of his killings was accelerating.

On July 13, 1991, he took Barbara Jacobs back to East Meadow and murdered her, not bothering to dismember the body this time, dropping her in the Hudson River. Then, on September 1, he strangled 22-year-old Mary Ellen DeLuca to death in a motel room. Rifkin claims he asked Mary Ellen if she wanted to die, prior to strangling her. She said yes, and he obliged her.

But he now needed to dispose of the body, and remembering a scene from another Hitchcock movie, he bought a steamer trunk, squeezed Mary Ellen's body into it, then drove to a rest stop near Cornwall, and dumped it there.

Also in September, he killed 31-year-old Yun Lee, strangling her in his car then dropping her body in the East River. Rifkin's selection pattern was somewhat erratic. He visited prostitutes virtually every night, leaving most of them unharmed, killing on a whim when the need took him. He'd been with Lee before, and he expressed remorse at her death, saying he had liked her.

Victim number six was killed just before Christmas 1991. Rifkin claims he can't remember her name, but the murder stands out in one respect. It provided him with a new method of disposal. After killing the woman, he drove to a recycling plant in Westbury, where he'd once worked. There he found a 55-gallon oil drum, pushed the body inside, then rolled it into the East River. Rifkin was about to leave the site when he was confronted by a couple of patrolmen who accused him of illegal dumping. Joel said that he was collected scrap metal. The officers believed him and let him go.

The oil drum had worked so well that Rifkin bought several more to use in dumping his victims. Next to die was Lorraine Orvieto, killed on December 26, then a week later, Mary Ann Holloman. Both were placed in drums and dispatched to the depths of the waterways around Manhattan.

By this time, many of the corpses had started turning up, leading the authorities to suspect that there might be a serial killer at work. But with 2,000 homicides a year, the police had their hands full and junkie prostitutes did not exactly rank high on their list of priorities. It was a serial killer's dream. Rifkin continued to murder at will.

Victim number nine was killed in May 1992, and dropped in Brooklyn's Newtown Creek. Also in May, Rifkin killed Ana Lopez. A month later, he murdered Iris Sanchez, a 25-year-old crack addict.

In August, Violet O'Neill went with Rifkin back to his house in East Meadow and ended up strangled and dismembered and later dumped in the Hudson River. In October, Rifkin strangled Mary Catherine Williams to death and in November, Jenny Soto. And the new year brought no respite for Manhattan's set-upon prostitutes. Leah Evens was killed on February 27, Lauren Marquez on April 2, 1993.

Rifkin's final victim - the one he'd been transporting when he was caught - was Tiffany Bresciani. He picked her up in the early hours of June 24, 1993, and drove her to a parking lot, where he strangled her. Then he headed back to East Meadow with the victim lying across the back seat. Stopping on the way, he bought rope and a tarp, which he used to wrap the body. He then moved it to the trunk.

When Rifkin arrived home, he found his mother waiting impatiently for him. She demanded her car keys and, before he could protest, she took them and drove off. Jeanne Rifkin returned from her shopping excursion 30 minutes later. Thankfully, she'd placed her shopping bags on the back seat. Had she popped the trunk, she'd have gotten the shock of her life.

As soon as it was convenient, Rifkin moved the body from the car to the garage where it remained for three days in the summer heat until the stench forced him to move it. His truck was being repaired at the time and wasn't roadworthy, but with his mother using the car, Rifkin was left with no choice. He'd bundled the corpse into the truck bed, covered it with the tarp and driven off, not even realizing that there was no license plate on the vehicle. That oversight had led directly to his arrest.

Rifkin's first trial, for the murder of Tiffany Bresciani, started on April 11, 1994. The basis of the prosecution's case was Rifkin's detailed confession to all 17 murders. This interview had not been recorded and was given in the absence of counsel, and the defense fought hard to suppress it. When the judge rejected their plea, the outcome of the case was all but a forgone conclusion. Rifkin was found guilty and sentenced to 25 years to life.

Following that conviction, he stood trial in Suffolk County on May 9, 1994, for the Evens and Marquez slayings, then in Queens and Brooklyn for the murders committed there. Found guilty on those charges he received numerous life sentences.

In 2002, New York's Supreme Court rejected Rifkin's appeal of his convictions. He is now serving 203 years to life in the Clinton Correctional Facility. He will, theoretically, be eligible for parole in 2197.

Arthur Shawcross

The Genesee River Strangler

On March 24, 1988, police were called to an area of Salmon Creek, a tributary of the Genesee River, outside Rochester, New York. Upon arrival, they were pointed to a figure in the water, a woman wearing jeans and a sweatshirt. As the body was brought to the shore, it was immediately clear that the woman had met with foul play. An autopsy would later prove this to be true. The woman had suffered a severe beating prior to her death, with vaginal trauma and bite marks. She'd also been strangled.

An identification wasn't long in coming. She was Dorothy "Dotsie" Blackburn, 27, a prostitute who worked the strip along Rochester's seedy Lyell Avenue. She'd last been seen alive on March 18.

Prostitution is a high-risk occupation and prostitute murders a fact of life for most city police departments. Rochester PD did what they could, but the meager leads they had led nowhere. A year passed without any progress, the case went cold. But then other prostitutes started showing up dead.

On September 9, a man, out searching for empty bottles, spotted a bone sticking out of the ground. At first, he was sure that it was from a dead animal, but then he noticed clothing scattered around the area and decided to call the police.

The body was severely decomposed, so it was impossible to determine how she'd died or even who she was. In order to aid in the latter, the police hired William Rodriguez III, a forensic anthropologist who did a clay reconstruction of the victim's face. This long complicated process involves building up a probable likeness based on the bone structure of the skull. The result was photographed and published in the local papers. Not long after, police received a call from a distressed father who identified the face as his daughter, Anna Steffen. Dental records later confirmed the identification.

Anna Steffen's body had been found some distance from Dorothy Blackburn's, so there was no reason for police to make a connection. Not yet.

Then, on Saturday, October 21, three hikers walking a trail along the Genesee River Gorge came across a decomposing, headless corpse. As police arrived to process the scene and remove the body, they had no idea that the killer was close by, standing on the opposite bank of the river, pretending to be an ordinary fisherman.

Six days later, a boy retrieving a ball at a site close to the Gorge, saw a foot sticking out from beneath a pile of debris. Police arrived to find the maggot-infested corpse of Patty Ives, a once-attractive Lyell Avenue prostitute.

The discovery of three dead prostitutes in such quick succession, made police sit up and take notice. Although there was still no solid evidence linking the deaths, they believed there might be a serial killer at work. The press certainly had no doubt about it. They began trumpeting headlines about the "Rochester Strangler" and "The Genesee River Killer." The pressure was now on the police to catch the murderer.

Since they had no viable suspects and no leads to follow, investigators focused their attention first on the killer's favored prey. Lyell Avenue was the preferred prostitute pick-up spot in Rochester, so they got vice officers on the ground talking to hookers and seeing if that turned up anything. In the meanwhile, police staked out the area in unmarked cars, while assuring the women that they'd turn a blind eye to their activities for now.

It was an uneasy truce, but the hookers felt safer for it. Some of them, though, insisted that they didn't need protecting. Julie Cicero, a tough, streetwise pro, carried a knife and wasn't afraid to use it. She insisted that the killer should be more afraid of her than she of him.

Another prostitute, Jo Ann Van Nostrand, described a frightening date she'd had with a man named "Mitch," who had insisted on driving her to a spot some distance from her normal haunts. There had been something strange about him, she said. For one thing, he mentioned the strangler several times. Then, he asked her to "play dead" while he had sex with her. That had made her nervous, so she'd told him that she had a knife and would use it if he tried anything funny. He'd told her he understood, but while they were together he'd tried several times to put his hands on her throat.

The story was potentially a lead, but as Jo Ann knew nothing more about Mitch, it was impossible to follow up. Instead, the police beefed up their surveillance and warned the women to be careful and to report any suspicious activity. But still prostitutes were going missing.

Maria Welch was a petite, pretty blonde who disappeared in November. When a body matching her description was discovered in the Gorge a few days later, investigators were sure it was Maria. They were wrong. It was a prostitute named Frances Brown who had last been seen getting into a car with a heavy-set man. Brown had been strangled to death after suffering a savage beating.

Not long after, a man called in at a Rochester police precinct to report his 26-year-old girlfriend missing. She had been gone for 18 days, he said, but he hadn't filed a report earlier because she often took off without notice. Her name was June Stott. Officers recorded it as a missing persons case, but as Stott wasn't a prostitute, they didn't link it to the Genesee River killer.

On November 15, Kimberly Logan, a black prostitute, well known in the Lyell Avenue area, was found dead beneath a pile of leaves in someone's yard. She'd been viciously beaten and kicked and leaves had been stuffed down her throat. Her file was added to the growing list of prostitute murders in the Rochester area.

Eight days later, a man out walking his dog discovered a corpse concealed under a strip of carpet. When investigators reached the scene, they found a woman lying face down on the ground. The corpse had been somewhat preserved by the cold weather but officers could see what appeared to be widespread bruising on her back. This, the medical examiner explained, was due to the blood pooling after death. She'd originally been laid on her back, and had spent some time in that position. That, in turn, meant that the killer had later returned to flip her over onto her face.

Her position suggested that she'd been anally penetrated after death. Then, as officers turned the body over, they discovered another sickening perversion – the woman had been cut open from her breasts to her vagina, and her vaginal lips had been removed.

The victim was soon identified as the missing June Stott, and her discovery posed a plethora of new question for the investigative team. Stott wasn't a prostitute and she'd suffered mutilations not seen in the other victims. Was she part of the same series, or was this something different entirely? With eleven unsolved homicides on their hands, Rochester PD decided it was time to call in the FBI.

Special Agent Gregg McCrary, of the Bureau's famed Behavioral Science Unit, was assigned to the case. He, in turn, invited New York State Trooper, Lieutenant Ed Grant (a graduate of the FBI's training program) to participate in the investigation. By the time they arrived in Rochester on December 13, another victim, Elizabeth Gibson, had been added to the killer's growing roster.

McCrary and Grant arrived quickly got to work, starting on Lyell Avenue and then visiting the crime scenes and going over the case files. They decided to sort the files into three groups, those they felt were linked to the Genesee River killer, those that might be linked, and those that were not linked. After some thought, they placed June Stott in the first group.

A profile was developed, describing the offender as a white male in his twenties to early thirties. He would have a criminal record, most likely for sexual offenses. He'd probably be a hunter or fisherman. He'd be friendly and approachable and wouldn't stand out in any way – a normal guy, driving an ordinary car, dressing in functional clothes. He'd work at a menial job, earning a low income. He'd have a wife or girlfriend. But for the age, this profile would prove to be uncannily accurate.

The FBI agent also suggested some investigative strategies. He believed that the killer might hang out in coffee shops or bars frequented by cops and that he might even be known to police. He also suggested that they put surveillance on any corpse found in the future, as the killer seemed to be revisiting his kills.

At the same time, a computer search, based on the profile McCrary and Grant had developed, offered up a promising suspect. However, the man's alibis for most of the murders checked out. It was back to square one.

The weeks before New Year brought two more missing prostitutes, Darlene Trippi and June Cicero, the tough, streetwise hooker who had told investigators that the killer ought to be afraid of her. Then, when a black streetwalker named Felicia Stephens also disappeared, police decided it was time to scour the Gorge from helicopters to see if they could find any likely dumpsites.

After three days of searching all they'd found was some clothing scattered along the side of the road near Salmon Creek, together with an ID card belonging to Felicia Stephens.

On January 3, 1990, a team working along Highway 31 spotted something lying on the icy surface of Salmon Creek, near a bridge. As they flew in closer, they saw that it was a woman's body dressed in jeans and a white hooded top. They were about to call it in, when they noticed a man standing on the bridge, looking towards where the body lay.

The man was tall and heavy-set and he appeared to be relieving himself. Then he walked casually away and got into his car – a Chevy Celebrity – and drove off. The helicopter unit alerted their colleagues on the ground and they set off in pursuit of the Chevy while the chopper kept it under surveillance from the air. Eventually, the vehicle pulled into a municipal parking lot in Spencerport and officers moved in to question the man.

He said that his name was Arthur John Shawcross and that he thought that the officers were following him because he'd urinated off the bridge. When asked for his driver's license, he admitted that he didn't have one and also confessed that he was an ex-felon, having served time for manslaughter.

The officers then asked Shawcross to accompany them to State Police Barracks for further questioning, which he agreed to willingly. He even signed forms giving them permission to search his house and car.

Shawcross remained under interrogation for five hours. At first, he was coy, telling investigators about his favorite fishing spots (which happened to be close to where many of the bodies were discovered). Asked about his manslaughter charge he said simply, "two kids died." However, as the interrogation proceeded, he opened up, talking about his experiences in Vietnam and eventually providing details about his previous conviction.

With sickening nonchalance, he told the officers that he'd killed a ten-year-old boy and an eight-year-old girl, sodomizing the latter before he strangled her. He'd served 14 years for the crimes. Asked again about his presence at Salmon Creek, he insisted that it was purely coincidental. He said he'd been out for a drive and had stopped to take a leak. He knew nothing about murdered prostitutes.

Officers were sure that Shawcross was lying, but with no evidence, they were forced to release him. Before he left, they asked if they could take his photograph. Shawcross agreed to it.

The task force now moved into overdrive, checking Shawcross' background. They discovered details of the murders he'd committed in Watertown, New York in 1972 - the murder of ten-year-old Jack Blake and the rape-murder of eight-year-old Karen Ann Hill. Under a plea bargain, he'd been allowed to plead guilty to manslaughter in the Hill murder and had received 25 years, while the charges relating to Black had been dropped. With time off for good behavior, Shawcross was back on the street in just over 14 years.

One detail in the crime scene report relating to the Hill murder jumped out at the detectives. Leaves had been forced down the little girl's throat. They'd seen the same thing in some of the Genesee River victims.

With that tenuous link between the two series, investigators decided to bring Shawcross in for a second round of questioning. This time, they drove him out to several of the crime scenes, while continuing to press him for details of the murders.

But Shawcross wouldn't budge, steadfastly maintaining his innocence. Then, as the interrogation became more heated, he asked to terminate it. He said that he needed to get home as he was worried about his girlfriend, Clara Neal, whose Chevy Celebrity he'd been driving when he was spotted on the bridge. One of the interrogating officers saw an opportunity and immediately seized upon it.

"Is Clara involved?" he asked.

"No," Shawcross said emphatically.

"But if you were using her car, she must have known about the murders," the officer insisted.

"Clara's not involved," Shawcross said, hanging his head. Within the next minute, the floodgates opened and he began recounting his sordid tale of murder and mutilation.

In true serial killer fashion, Shawcross offered a justification for each of the killings – some of them had ridiculed him, others had tried to steal from him, some had threatened to tell Clara that he was seeing prostitutes, one had bitten his penis, another talked too much. As for his methods, he said that he smothered some victims and strangled others by pressing his arm down on their throats. The mutilation of June Stott was to "aid in decomposition," because he knew her and had "cared" about her. When his confession was finally transcribed, it ran to 79 pages.

Arthur Shawcross went on trial in November 1990. Despite an ill-advised attempt at an insanity defense, he was found guilty on ten charges of first-degree murder and sentenced to 25 years on each charge, for a total of 250 years.

But Shawcross would serve only eighteen of those years. On the afternoon of November 10, 2008, Shawcross complained to a guard about pains in his leg. He was taken to Albany Medical Center, where he suffered a fatal heart attack at 9:50 p.m. Few, if any, mourned his passing.

Coral Eugene Watts

The Sunday Morning Slasher

"She had evil eyes. I was trying to release her spirit." – Coral Watts

In May 1982, Lori Lister, 21, arrived at her apartment in Houston, Texas after visiting her boyfriend. As she parked her car and walked towards the front door of her building, she was probably unaware that she was being followed. But a man was tracking her, and as she slotted her key into the front door, he came up quickly behind her and put his hands on her neck. Lori's screams were quickly cut off as the man increased pressure on her throat. She felt the light fading, she was sure that she was going to die.

Fortunately for Lori, her muffled cries had been heard by a neighbor, who was on the phone to the police, even as the attacker dragged Lori inside. As the man eased Lori to the floor, he encountered her roommate, 18-year-old Melinda Aguilar. He threatened to slash Melinda's throat if she screamed, then choked her into submission. Fearing for her life, Melinda decided to play dead. It worked. The attacker lowered her to the carpet then began binding the girls' hands with coat hangers. That completed, he did a peculiar thing. He was so excited to have control over the two women that he jumped up and down, clapping his hands like some fairy tale ogre. He then walked to the bathroom and began filling the tub.

Melinda waited until he was out of sight, then staggered to her feet and crossed the room to the second-floor balcony. She clambered over the railing and dropped to the ground, screaming for all she was worth, hoping it wasn't too late to save her friend's life. Moments later, a police car screeched to a halt outside the building.

Hearing the sirens, the intruder tried to flee but the police officers cut off his escape and apprehended him in the courtyard. Meanwhile, the neighbor who had called the police rushed to Lori and Melissa's apartment. He was just in time to pull Lori from the tub, where the intruder had been trying to drown her.

Investigators soon identified the attacker as Coral Eugene Watts. Asked why he had tried to kill the women, Watts said that they had "evil eyes" and that he was trying to "release their spirits." He also told officers that he had done it before – at least 80 times.

Carl Eugene Watts was born on November 7, 1953, in Killeen, Texas. His father, Richard, was a soldier, based at Fort Hood at the time of Carl's birth. His mother, Dorothy Mae, was a teacher. Just days after Carl was born, the couple moved back to their hometown of Coalwood, West Virginia. A year later their second child, Sharon, was born.

Richard and Dorothy Mae had been childhood sweethearts, but their marriage was an unhappy one that eventually ended in divorce in 1955. Following the breakup, Dorothy Mae moved with her two children to Inkster, Michigan, where she found work as a high school art teacher. But the family would regularly return to Coalwood to visit relatives, and Carl loved the southern town so much that he later changed his name to Coral - a southern pronunciation of his name.

In 1962, Coral's mother re-married, a situation that greatly distressed the boy, partly because he didn't like his new stepfather and partly because he hated having a competitor for his mother's affections.

Around this time, another life-changing event occurred in his life. He developed meningitis, his temperature running so high that doctors feared it might have caused brain damage. Coral recovered, but it seemed that the doctors' assessment had been right. There were changes to his behavior, subtle at first, but plain to see for all who knew him.

The first sign was in his academic performance. Coral had missed a year of school due to his illness and was held back a grade when he returned. But the formerly bright student had difficulty concentrating and his grades began to slip, leaving his mother to wonder how badly his illness had affected him.

Then there were the dreams, violent dramas in which he tussled with the evil spirits of women and killed them. More worrying was his assessment of these nightmares. They didn't frighten him, the young boy declared, in fact, he enjoyed them.

If his parents took this as a warning sign as to the state of his mental health they appear to have taken no action until, inevitably, his fantasies manifested in reality. In 1968, when Coral was 15, he knocked on the door of a 26-year-old woman named Joan Gave. When Mrs. Gave answered the door, Coral forced her back into her apartment, pushed her to the floor and started beating her. When he was done, he left her apartment and continued his newspaper delivery route as if nothing had happened.

Gave immediately called the police, and they were waiting for Coral when he returned home. Brought before a judge, he was ordered to undergo psychiatric treatment at the Lafayette Clinic in Detroit. Here, psychiatrists diagnosed him with strong homicidal tendencies and flagged him as a danger to others. Nonetheless, the boy was released just a few months later, on his 16th birthday.

He was ordered to undergo outpatient treatment, which amounted to just nine subsequent consultations.

Coral returned to school, where his academic performance remained poor. He excelled, though, at sports, particularly football and boxing, which allowed him to release his pent-up aggression.

With extensive tutoring by his mother, he graduated high school at age 19, and despite his low grade point average, he won a football scholarship to Lane College in Jackson, Tennessee. However, he remained at school only a few months before returning home. He said that it was due to a leg injury that prevented him from playing football. More likely, he just couldn't bear to be away from his mother.

Back in Michigan, Watts found work as an apprentice mechanic in Detroit, remaining at that trade for a year before enrolling at Western Michigan University in Kalamazoo. Soon after, there were a rash of attacks in the area around the campus - one of them fatal.

On October 25, 1974, Lenore Knizacky, 23, heard a knock at her front door. When she answered it, there was a young black man standing there. He said he was looking for someone named

Charles, but before she could answer he grabbed her by the throat and forced her into the apartment. He began strangling her, but she managed to fight him off, forcing him to flee.

Five days later, on October 30, 19-year old Gloria Steele opened her door to a man who said he was looking for Charles. The man forced his way in and attacked Gloria with a knife, stabbing her 33 times.

The man tried the same ruse with another student on November 12. Fortunately, she was able to escape and as the man fled the scene and jumped into his vehicle, she noted down his license plate number. Police followed up. The car belonged to Coral Eugene Watts.

Watts was soon in custody on two charges of battery and he readily admitted the charges, even adding that he'd attacked at least a dozen more women. He balked though when confronted with the murder of Gloria Steele, insisting that he hadn't killed anyone.

As a precursor to his court hearing, Watts was ordered to undergo a psychiatric evaluation at Kalamazoo State Hospital. Psychiatrists there found that he was emotionally detached and lacked remorse for his actions. They diagnosed him with an antisocial personality disorder but insisted that he was well aware of the difference between right and wrong and, therefore, competent to stand trial.

Watts would spend six months under psychiatric care during which time he suffered from depression and made a half-hearted attempt at suicide. When his case eventually came to trial in the summer of 1975, he was sentenced to a year in jail on the battery charges. Unfortunately, he was never charged with the murder of Gloria Steele because prosecutors lacked the evidence to convict him. If they had, an awful lot of lives might have been saved.

After Watts was released in 1976, he found work as a mechanic and returned to live with his mother. Those who knew him described him as a "mama's boy" because he didn't like being away from his mother. The other women in his life just didn't measure up.

But that is not to say that there weren't other women. Shortly after his release from prison, Watts began seeing a woman named Delores, fathering a child by her before they split. He then started dating another woman, Valeria, who he married in 1979. The marriage lasted just six months before Valeria walked out, mainly due to Coral's bizarre conduct.

Years later, Valeria would describe some of his behaviors to investigators. She said that he suffered violent nightmares, would throw garbage on the floor, would slash at houseplants with a knife and melt candles into the furniture. She also said that, immediately after they had sex, Watts would leave the house and stay away for several hours.

Watts never explained where he went on these occasions, but investigators were able to provide a ready explanation. They believed that Watts was out stalking victims. Several women were attacked and murdered during this period, in attacks bearing Watts' unique signature.

One of those attacks occurred on Halloween 1979. Detroit News reporter Jeanne Clyne, 44, was attacked as she walked home from a doctor's appointment. She died from 11 stab wounds, inflicted on a busy suburban road, in broad daylight.

Then, on April 20, high school student Shirley Small was killed by two knife wounds to the heart, outside her home in Ann Arbor, Michigan. Another Ann Arbor woman perished in a similar attack. Glenda Richmond, 26, was stabbed 28 times, outside the diner that she managed. And an even more frenzied attack occurred on

September 14. University of Michigan graduate student, Rebecca Huff, 20, suffered at least 50 knife wounds.

In the wake of the Huff murder, a task force was formed to investigate the recent spate of homicides in the area. Under the leadership of Detective Paul Bunten, the task force soon identified Watts as a suspect and brought him in on a warrant to provide a blood sample. Bunten had hoped that he might coax a confession out of Watts, but Watts wasn't talking. Neither did the blood sample connect him to any crime.

Annoyed by the police attention, Watts decided to leave town, relocating to Columbus, Texas, where he found work at an oil company. Columbus is just 70 miles from Houston. Soon Coral Watts took to cruising that city, looking for new victims.

But Paul Bunten wasn't about to let Watts' off the hook that easily. As soon as he heard about the move, he contacted the Houston police to warn them about the serial killer who had just arrived in their city. He even sent them copies of his files on Watts, in the hope of preventing more murders.

Houston PD, however, had been unable to locate Watts, and the warning from Bunten was soon forgotten. It would remain so until the attack on Lori Lister and Melinda Aguilar in May 1982. Now under arrest for those crimes, Watts clammed up and refused to talk. His refusal drove Harris County Assistant District Attorney Ira Jones, to offer an extraordinary deal. He promised Watts immunity on any murder charges he confessed to.

One of America's most horrendous serial killers had just been given the equivalent of a get-out-of-jail-free card, and unsurprisingly, Watts took the deal. On August 9, 1982, he confessed to 13 murders. He hinted that he might have been the man responsible for the 1979 Detroit murder of Jeanne Clyne but insisted that he hadn't killed Glenda Richard, Shirley Small or Rebecca Huff (even though there was strong physical and circumstantial evidence linking him to those crimes). As to his Houston victims, he confessed to drowning University of Texas student Linda Tilley, 22, in her apartment complex swimming pool in September 1981. He also admitted to stabbing 25-year-old Elizabeth Montgomery to death, one week later.

The same day, he killed Susan Wolf, 21, stabbing her to death as she returned from the grocery store. In January 1982, he strangled 27-year-old Phyllis Tamm, while she was out jogging. Two days later, he murdered architecture student Margaret Fossi, 25. Her body was later found in the trunk of her car at Rice University.

During that month, Watts attacked three more Houston women, slashing one across the throat, stabbing one with a knife and another with an ice pick. Miraculously, all three survived.

His next victims were not as lucky. Between February and May 1982, Watts killed Elena Semander, 20; Emily LaQua, 14; Anna Ledet, 34; Yolanda Gracia, 21; Carrie Jefferson, 32; Suzanne Searles, 25, and Michele Maday, 20.

He admitted to at least 80 more murders in Michigan and Canada but refused to give any details, because his immunity deal only applied to the murders committed in Texas.

Eventually brought to trial for the attack on Lori Lister and Melinda Aguilar, Watts pled guilty to one count of burglary with intent to kill, the plea bargain he'd agreed. He was sentenced to 60 years in prison, parting with these chilling words, "You know, if they ever let me out, I'll kill again."

And Watts may well have had the opportunity to make good on his threat. In 1989, the Texas Court of Criminal Appeals ruled that the judge had failed to inform Watts that the bathtub he'd attempted to drown Lori Lister in was construed as a lethal weapon. Consequently, he was now considered a "non-violent" inmate and would not be required to serve his full term. The man who had sworn that he would kill again if he ever got out, was due for mandatory parole on May 9, 2006.

It was a terrifying thought and as the date grew closer, authorities in Michigan and Texas were desperate for any reason to keep Coral Watts behind bars. They began revisiting old cases, searching for evidence that might have been overlooked, evidence that might be used to keep Coral Watts off the streets. They eventually found it in the 1979 murder of Helen Mae Dutcher.

Dutcher had been attacked in an alleyway outside a Ferndale, Michigan, dry cleaning establishment and had been stabbed 12 times in the neck and back. An eyewitness, Joseph Foy, had reported the murder, but the police hadn't been able to catch the attacker, even though the composite gleaned from Foy's description strongly resembled Watts.

In 2004, Foy saw a television program regarding the Watts case and again contacted police. It was the break investigators had been waiting for. With an eyewitness to the murder, they filed new charges against Watts.

Coral Watts was extradited to Michigan in April 2004. His trial began in November and ended with a guilty verdict for first-degree murder. Because Michigan doesn't have the death penalty, Watts was sentenced to life imprisonment without the possibility of parole. He died in prison on Friday, September 21, 2007, of prostate cancer. He was 53 years old.

What Makes A Serial Killer?

"I don't march to the same drummer you do." – Convicted killer Douglas Clark a.k.a. The Sunset Strip Slayer

What makes a serial killer? Is there something unique in their genetic make-up, their physiology, thought patterns, or upbringing? Do they lack morality or social programming? Are they unable to control their rage and sexual urges? Are they mad or bad? What sets them apart?

These questions have vexed criminologists, profilers, psychologists, and forensic psychiatrists for decades. They've been the subject of countless studies and dissertations. They've formed the basis of thousands of man-hours worth of interviews and investigation. And yet, definitive answers remain elusive.

Serial killers themselves have offered some suggestions. Henry Lee Lucas blamed his upbringing; Jeffrey Dahmer said that he was born with a part of him missing; Ted Bundy blamed pornography; Herbert Mullin, said it was voices in his head ordering him to kill; Kenneth Bianchi blamed an alter-ego, while Bobby Joe Long said a motorcycle accident turned him into a serial sex killer. Some, like John Wayne Gacy, even had the temerity to blame their victims.

As for the rest of us, we console ourselves that they must be insane. After all, what sane person could slaughter another for pleasure? What normal person could perpetuate the atrocities that serial killers do, and repeat them again and again?

Yet the most terrifying thing about serial killers is that they are not shambling, jabbering ogres, but rational and calculating, impossible to tell from the general populace until it's too late.

So what exactly is a serial killer?

The National Institutes of Justice define serial murder as;

"A series of two or more murders committed as separate events, usually, but not always, by one offender acting alone. The crimes may occur over a period of time, ranging from hours to years. Quite often the motive is psychological, and the offender's behavior and the physical evidence observed at the crime scene will reflect sadistic, sexual overtones."

And the FBI's Behavioral Science Unit provides us with some traits common in serial killers.

They are typically white males in their twenties and thirties.

They are usually quite smart, with an IQ designated, "bright normal."

Despite their intelligence, they are underachievers, often doing poorly at school, and ending up in unskilled employment.

They often come from broken homes with an absent father and domineering mother. Some are adopted. Often, there is a history of psychiatric problems, criminality, and substance abuse in their families.

Many were physically, psychological and/or sexually abused in childhood. Some have suffered head trauma due to abuse or accident.

In adolescence, many of them wet the bed, started fires, and tortured animals.

They have problems with male authority figures and strong hostility towards women.

They manifest psychological problems at an early age. Many have spent time in institutions as children.

They have a general hatred towards humanity, including themselves. Some report suicidal thoughts as teenagers.

They display an interest in sex at an unnaturally young age. As they mature this interest becomes obsessive and turns towards fetishism, voyeurism, and violent pornography.

A Façade of Normality

The traits listed above might incline you to believe that you'd be able to spot a serial killer a mile off, but the frightening truth is that they are masters at camouflage, deceit, and deception. They know exactly how to blend in, how to avert your suspicions, how to put you at ease. They are the charming stranger who strikes up a conversation with you on the bus, the lost driver who courteously asks for directions, the man hobbling on a cane who politely asks for your help.

Like all skilled predators, they can sniff out the slightest hint of an opportunity, they know who to target and how to stalk. Being psychologically vacant they are adept at assuming whatever role they need, and that role will be the one required to snare their victim. To quote serial killer, Henry Lee Lucas, "it's like being a movie star... you're just playing the part."

Is serial murder a recent phenomenon?

Since we're trying to understand what makes a serial killer, this is a valid question, and the answer depends who you're listening to, because there are two distinct schools of thought. One believes that societal influences since just before the turn of the 20th century (and especially since WWII) have created the perfect conditions for the emergence of serial killers. They point to serial killers as a symptom of crowded rat syndrome, a product of class struggle and a manifestation of our attitudes towards sex.

The only problem with this argument is that it suggests that serial killers are purely a product of their environment. I consider that unlikely and am more inclined towards the second hypothesis, which holds that serial killers have always lived among us.

Adherents to this belief point to acts of human barbarism throughout history, from the terrible legends that appear in folklore, to the crimes of Gilles de Rais and Elizabeth Bathory, to the vicious outlaws and desperados of the Old West. They regard tales of werewolves, vampires, and man-eating trolls, as attempts by our less sophisticated ancestors to make sense of the hideous crimes committed by historical serial killers. A number of these legendary monsters, like the German "werewolf" Peter Stubbe and his French counterpart, Gilles Garnier, were in fact captured and put to death. They proved to be, not lycanthropes, but all too human monsters, serial killers, in fact.

What makes a serial killer?

No single cause will ever provide an answer as to why serial killers are driven to commit murder again and again. Rather a combination of factors, physiological, psychological, and environmental, must be in play. Nonetheless, we can look at the known commonalities in captured serial killers and draw some conclusions. Is this a comprehensive list? Hardly. We simply don't have the knowledge to solve the enigma of the serial killer.

Psychopaths

All serial killers, except perhaps for the small minority that are genuinely psychotic, are psychopaths. They would not be able to commit their horrendous crimes otherwise. Psychopaths are characterized by their irrationally antisocial behavior, their lack of conscience, their emotional emptiness, and their appetite for risk, all of which could easily be applied to serial killers.

Lacking in empathy, they have no problem in turning their victims into objects, there to be exploited and manipulated. Being devoid of emotions (in the way that you and I would understand them) they are like a blank screen, onto which can be projected whatever suits their needs in the moment. This is what makes them so good at play acting and manipulation.

Being compulsive thrill seekers, they are literally fearless, sometimes abducting victims in broad daylight, or with clear risk of discovery. This thrill seeking behavior also means that they are less easily stimulated than normal people. They require higher levels of excitement to get their rocks off, even if it means murder and mayhem.

Does this mean that all psychopaths become serial killers? Absolutely not. Most psychopaths aren't even criminals. In fact, many excel in fields like business and political leadership. Not all psychopaths are serial killers, but all serial killers, most certainly, are psychopaths.

Sexual Deviance

A second factor that must be present in all serial killers is sexual deviance. Serial murders are by their nature, sex crimes. A sexual motive is a requisite in both the Institutes of Justice and FBI definitions and an examination of any serial murder (even those that appear to have a different motive) will undoubtedly prove that the killer achieved some form of sexual release in the commission of the crime.

According to Ressler, Burgess, and Douglas in Sexual Homicide: Patterns and Motives, there are two types of sexual homicide: "the rape or displaced anger murder" and the "sadistic, or lust murder."

For some murderers, the rape is the primary objective for the crime, the murder committed to cover it up. For others, the act of murder and the ritual acts associated with it, provide the sexual release. The annals of serial murder abound with such cases, Bundy, Kearney, Kemper, Nilsen and others were necrophiles; Rader, Kraft, Berdella et al. achieved sexual release through torture; others like Kroll and Fish, through cannibalism. Still others are aroused by stabbing or by the "intimate" act of strangulation.

And with serial killers this deviance usually manifests in childhood. Fledgling serial killers are often flashers, peeping toms, molesters of younger children, chronic masturbators, even, as in the case of Harvey Glatman, juvenile sadomasochists. And even if they're not committing sex crimes at a young age, they're thinking about them.

Other Common Factors

But even a psychopath with unusual sexual appetites won't necessarily become a serial killer. He might find a partner (or more likely, partners) to cater for his tastes, or he might visit prostitutes who will do the same for a price. He may turn his talents towards becoming a 'love 'em and leave 'em' pick-up artist.

No, something else needs to happen to push our young psychopath over the threshold. An additional X-factor, or factors, needs to be in place. Thanks to the work done by the FBI in interviews with captured serial murderers, we know what some of those factors are.

Born Bad

The idea that someone might be inherently evil would have been scoffed at not too long ago. However, as we begin to understand more about the unique reality that murderers inhabit, it becomes clear that their warped view of the world takes root at an early age.

"Trash Bag Killer" Patrick Kearney said that he knew from age 8 that he would kill people; Ed Kemper had a crush on his second grade teacher, but told a friend, "if I kiss her I would have to kill her first"; Ted Bundy was leaving butcher's knives in his aunt's bed at the age of just 3; John Joubert was slashing girls with a razor blade before he reached his teens; Harvey Glatman was practicing sadomasochism when he was only 4 years old.

Child Abuse

Not every abused child becomes a serial killer, but a disproportionately high number of serial killers suffered abuse as children. "Boston Strangler," Albert De Salvo's father was a particularly brutal man who regularly beat his wife and children with metal pipes, brought prostitutes home and even sold his children into slavery. Joseph Kallinger's mother forced him to hold his hand over a flame, and beat him if he cried. Henry Lee Lucas' mother beat him so hard she fractured his skull. She also forced the young boy to watch her having sex with men.

And yet, others serial killers grew up in seemingly normal homes - Jeffrey Dahmer, for example, or Joel Rifkin, or Patrick Kearney. Some, like "Pied Piper of Tucson," Charles Schmid, were even pampered and indulged, their every desire catered to.

Domineering Mothers

Many serial killers seem to come from a home with an absent or passive father figure, and a dominating mother. This was certainly the case with both Henry Lee Lucas and Ed Kemper, both of whom eventually murdered their mothers.

Joseph Kallinger's mother was a sadist; Ed Gein's a religious nut who constantly warned him of the dangers of sex. Bobby Joe Long's mother made him sleep in her bed until he was thirteen. Ed Kemper's mom locked him in the cellar because she said his large size frightened his sisters. Charles Manson's mother reportedly traded him for a pitcher of beer. And at the other end of the scale was "Hillside Strangler" Kenneth Bianchi's cloyingly overprotective mom.

Either way, dysfunctional mother/son relationships seem to be present in the upbringing of an alarmingly high number of serial killers.

Adoption

Millions of children are adopted every year and grow up to live normal, productive lives. But there are an unusually high percentage of serial killers who were given up by their birth mothers for adoption. David Berkowitz, Charles Schmid, Joel Rifkin, Kenneth Bianchi, and Joseph Kallinger (to name a few) all fall into this category.

Finding out that one was adopted can be devastating for any child, creating a sense of disconnect, an uncertainty over one's identity. And, in a child already suffering with other issues (such as some of those mentioned above), it can be particularly devastating, unleashing feelings of rejection and simmering anger.

Exposure To Violence

Some serial killers blame juvenile exposure to violence for their misdeeds. Ed Gein, for example, claimed that seeing farm animals slaughtered gave him perverted ideas, while both Albert Fish and Andrei Chikatilo blamed their brutal murders on frightening stories they were told as children. As a child, John George Haigh saw a man decapitated by a bomb during the London blitz in WWII. Richard Ramirez was only thirteen when his cousin committed a murder right in front of him (those who knew him at the time said he showed no emotion and continued to idolize his cousin).

Rejection by Peers

Many serial killers are outsiders and loners in childhood. The nerdy Joel Rifkin was picked on and bullied throughout his school years. Likewise, the diminutive and sickly Patrick Kearney. Henry Lee Lucas was ridiculed and ostracized because of his glass eye, Kenneth Bianchi because of his incontinence. Jeffrey Dahmer was deliberately antisocial as a kid, a teenaged alcoholic who laughed when he saw a classmate injured. Harvey Glatman preferred spending time alone in his room indulging in autoerotic strangulation.

Separated from their peers, these troubled youngsters begin to rely on fantasy to bridge the gap. Often these begin as "revenge fantasies" against those who have wronged them, like abusive parents or schoolyard bullies. The relief that these fantasies bring, leads to ever more violent daydreams, which may begin to manifest through two of the three "triad" behaviors, fire-starting and animal cruelty.

Fantasy

The role of fantasy in the metamorphosis of a killer has been extensively studied. All of us fantasize at some time, perhaps about asking a pretty girl out, or meeting our favorite celebrity or turning out for our favorite sports teams. The fantasies of a fledgling serial killer, though, are a deep and disturbing mix of murder, mutilation, and aberrant sex.

Serial killers will dwell on these fantasies (sometimes for years), deepening them and adding layers of detail. Eventually though, the fantasy will no longer be enough and they'll feel compelled to act, the pressure building until it is impossible to resist.

How long before fantasy manifests in reality? Peter Kurten, Jesse Pomeroy, and Mary Bell committed multiple murders as children, Yosemite killer, Cary Stayner, said that he'd fantasized about killing a woman for 30 years before he eventually followed through.

Brain Damage

Brain damage, especially to the hypothalamus, limbic region, and temporal lobe can cause severe behavioral changes, specifically as regards emotion, empathy, and aggression responses.

Many serial killers - Leonard Lake, David Berkowitz, Kenneth Bianchi, John Wayne Gacy, Carl Panzram, Henry Lee Lucas, Bobby Joe Long, among them - have suffered head injuries, either in accidents or in childhood beatings.

Others, Ted Bundy for example, have been subjected to extensive X-rays and brain scans, which revealed no evidence of brain damage or trauma. Neither does everyone who suffers head trauma become a killer. So while brain damage or dysfunction is undoubtedly a factor in the behavior of some serial killers, it is far from being a universal "kill switch."

Societal Influences

Psychopaths find it difficult to accept responsibility for their actions, so it is unsurprising that many serial killers blame society for their acts. The poster boy for this theory is Ted Bundy. Bundy has spoken at length about the influence of violent pornography on the killer that he became.

Is there any validity to his claims?

We do seem to be a society that glorifies violence, from live footage of bombs falling on Baghdad, to movies in which the hero is every bit as violent as the bad guy he's trying to defeat. Porn, too, is easily available, both online and in movies and magazines. But neither of these provides a rationale for serial murder. If everyone who watched a Rambo movie or downloaded porn were to become a serial killer we'd have an epidemic on our hands.

Conclusion

At the beginning of the article I asked, "What makes a serial killer?" The reasons may be more complex than we think, perhaps beyond our comprehension. A better question to ask may be, "Is anyone capable of serial murder?" And the answer to that is an emphatic "No!"

The creation of a serial killer requires a perfect (or more appropriately, an imperfect) storm, whereby some of the factors mention above, and perhaps some others that are not, are blended together into a toxic brew with psychopathy and sexual deviance.

A combination of aberrant psychology, childhood abuse, and peer rejection leading to the development of fantasies that involve death and sex and then manifest in fire-starting and animal cruelty, can hardly fail to produce someone who, given the opportunity, will kill and kill again.

For more True Crime books by Robert Keller please visit

http://bit.ly/kellerbooks

Printed in Great Britain
by Amazon